Collection International Law

Directed by
Margherita Salvadori

Edited by
Carlos Antonio Agurto Gonzáles
Sonia Lidia Quequejana Mamani
Benigno Choque Cuenca
Miriam Milagros Albites Palomino

Luis Manuel Marcano Salazar

Fundamentals of Public International Law

Introduction to the study of Public International Law Institutions' history and its impact on International Relations

Edited by
Carlos Antonio Agurto Gonzáles
Sonia Lidia Quequejana Mamani
Benigno Choque Cuenca

Ediciones Olejnik

Title of a book: FUNDAMENTALS OF PUBLIC INTERNATIONAL LAW. INTRODUCTION TO THE STUDY OF PUBLIC INTERNATIONAL LAW INSTITUTIONS' HISTORY AND ITS IMPACT ON INTERNATIONAL RELATIONS

Huérfanos 611, Santiago - Chile
E-mail: contacto@edicionesolejnik.com
Web site: http://www.edicionesolejnik.com

Primera edición en Ediciones Olejnik: 2020

ISBN: 978-956-392-775-7

Diseño de Carátula: Ena Zuñiga
Diagramación: Luis A. Sierra Cárdenas

Impreso en Argentina 2020 Printed in Argentina

TABLET OF CONTENTS

CHAPTER IV
LATIN-AMERICAN LEGAL FOUNDATION

CHAPTER V
THE INTERNATIONAL COMMUNITY

CHAPTER VI
FOREIGN POLICY AND INTERNATIONAL LAW

PROLOGUE

During my 30-year-carrer, as a Foreign Service officer, I have dealt with realities, situations, conflicts, bilateral agreements and multilateral treaties, in which International Law as a reference has been fundamental, not only in the conceptual traditional structure but also in the regulation response to the complexity and dynamism of the International System. As a professor of this subject in different Venezuelan universities, I have dealt with International Law classic books -foreign and national ones- in which the teaching and learning process in this field is not updated in their syllabus regarding the ongoing reality of the international circumstance.

That is why it has been an honor and a great satisfaction to me to respond to Doctor Luis Manuel Marcano Salazar's request (a university professor and diplomatic colleague) which is to write the prologue of this Public International Law book that, headed to students and professors, gets us closer to International Law in an updated manner with the XXI century perspective. This book, besides letting ourselves memorize a few traditional concepts, allows ourselves to get closer to the current reality with analytical and synthetic spirit, in which knowledge constitute the main interest. But essentially it is to understand the international circumstance labyrinth.

Luis Manuel holds a solid legal, political and historical background. He is a Lawyer, Political Scientist and Historian. He has performed in the international sphere as a diplomatic officer and was my student in the Master of International Affairs of the Foreign Affairs Ministry, specifically in a course named «New World Order», which has been under my responsibility since I came back to Venezuela after my last position as Ambassador in Libya. In addition to this, he also holds an Expertise in International Relations from Universidad Central de Venezuela, a Master's degree in Political Science from Universidad Simon Bolivar and PhD in Political Science. I even played a part in the admission examinations and introductory workshop directed to the new Venezuelan Foreign Service officers, in which this young diplomat got a well-deserved first place.

This young and intellectual person labor goes further of what the title of this work represents itself, denominated by him Fundamentals of Public

International Law, which can be checked from the beginning of the first chapter by affirming that «the purpose of the Public International Law is dichotomous», based on the double role idea. As far as science is concerned -considered basic by us, as he affirms- it analyses the legal, social and economic principles, which determine the conversations and negotiations in its content, regarding the facts that characterize the new international order. As a discipline, Professor Luis Manuel Marcano Salazar affirms: «the required stability in the international community is regulated», it arises the idea that International Law has an indivisible characteristic and it is both a science and a discipline. But in the first chapter this lawyer goes further. He immediately analyses the evolution of Public International Law since the Antique age until the present-day, placing this science-discipline as a universal Public International Law and pointing out its interdisciplinary relations among other sciences.

Nowadays, the world has experienced major changes in the legal structure of Public International Law. In fact, when it comes to the internal laws of each State, those changes rise themselves indirectly as a result of an internal legislative body. On the other hand, the situation is different about Public International Law, since the influence of major changes creates new points of view on the political, economic, geographic and cultural matter, which are transferred to the legal international structure.

In fact, we all agree with him on the idea that Law has been intrinsic to social life and manhood. The rules have been present in mankind performance, starting with the very first social exhibitions until the computing and satellite era. Humankind development and progress have had the principles and rules as guidance to aim for a fair and stable existence. Law as project intended to settle order and based on values accepted by a community, is a merger element to give the idea of belonging to a group of people, a nation and the international society, in which the duties and rights are established, the contracts are accepted, infringements are punished and manhood behavior is established in a coercive manner but is also ruled by acknowledged values, legalized and in force. From the moment that communities began to establish relationships among each other (beyond their legal order) due to the linking factor of the foreign element, International Law, both Private (due to the relations between an individual and a variety of autonomous legal rules demanding the pursuit of justice, foreign rules and court decisions) and Public (with international rules and treaties, referred to relations among Nations-States and not among individuals, pertaining the cooperation, security and international peace) was born.

International Law is not a simple addition of legal-national rules, but an autonomous discipline, and that is the author points it out with a general point of view, based on the principles and rules with a universal characteristic to all States. The author has the quality for the management of the topic of the new Community Law, which goes beyond the State-Nation concept. Nowadays it is reality the concept of region-State, as well as International Integration Law and the supranational legal realities of the regional systems, such as the European Union, or sub-regional systems, such as the Andean Community-Mercosur.

These new geopolitical and geo-economics' realities accept rules that allow them integrate into national orders and are based on a common International Law. We could even talk about a Constitutional International Law. The author does not open up this argument but it can be inferred from the books and the topics. It is a motivation to specialists this necessary contribution and intellectual debate.

The author acknowledges the realistic approaching of the legal rule as guidance and mandate, but also the weakness of its structure and content regarding its mandatory fulfillment. He is separated from the utopic point of view and does not fall for the cynical attitude of the irrational power in the world. It is observed in his proposals the balance between the weakness and strength of International Law into the pursuit of individuals and nations in a new world order, based on liberty and justice not only in the national community but also in the world system.

Chapter II which deals with the foundations of the sources of Public International Law does not limit to naming them but also takes Hans Kelsen's definition of sources (1994) as the origin from which something is derived. That origin, of course, carries itself some specific and general aspects. In our foreign experience we have been able to prove this statement, as the specific is observed on the legal (the rules) and the diverse on the cultural aspects (custom). The author goes further when he analyses the different schools that sustain Public International Law and then goes deeper on the search of the sources themselves: international treaties, international custom, general principles of Law, doctrine, equality, unilateral acts of States, international organizations' resolutions, as well as the sources derived from scientific and technologic processes.

The author makes a detailed analysis about the diverse phases which treaties are subject to before approved, divided into two. He considers important the initial phase, which is split into «negotiation-adoption» and «authentication», and the final phase, split into «consent demonstration» and «consent signing». This process is denominated «form and substance conditions». In addition, the author sustains the «conclusion and entry in force» processes of the treaties, pointing out that «the closure of a treaty» is a negotiation process. This process is considered essential in the new international order to overcome the conflicts and possible wars, in which the role of the UN and a new global awareness will determine humankind survival.

Chapter III is essential to understand the real meaning of the strategic order that diplomacy represents. An important distinction is made regarding the negotiation process as a place in between persuasion and imposition. It is stated that negotiation needs the strength in order to «submit a subject or State to comply with the rules to be established unilaterally». Afterwards, it is quoted that negotiation is positioned in the political scope, in which concessions are made and flexibility is given in order to reach a satisfactory agreement for both parties.

Also, this intellectual young professor, deeply analyses the connection between Diplomatic Law and Foreign Policy. The latter is defined as a political action and public policy, and diplomacy as an action. Diplomatic Law is defined as legislative and legitimating body of the action of the State, and the diplomat is defined as an executor of the purposes of the State and interests of the foreign policy. Both are interesting and necessary distinctions to understanding the aspects chained to action-execution with the whole ruling system of Public International Law.

The author's academic experience, both undergraduate and master level, is expressed in this third chapter and all aspects related to diplomatic representations are fully detailed. On that matter, he begins with an important distinction between «political action» and «public policy», granting the latter a longer permanence on time. Afterwards, each fundamental topic is consolidated, such as diplomatic representations, diplomatic privileges and immunities, as well, as the Vienna Convention on Diplomatic Relations. The end of the chapter is dedicated to Consular Law, starting with a historic reference. It is verses on the consular service, which is considered very important for the commercial relations among the countries. Lastly, the author makes a deep analysis of the Organic Law on Foreign Service[1], in which the Consuls attributions, their immunities and consular prerogatives, patent letter and the Venezuelan Foreign Service are studied.

Chapter IV starts with the usage of «Venezuelan legal ground», and presents some interesting considerations about international society and Law. Positivist criteria is step aside as some items that may consider an enriched and widened international subjectivity are found, especially when it comes to determine the subjects of International Law. The author, in this field, quotes the conceptual review of Antonio Brotons (1997). He also raises the rejections that question of the enforceability of International Law. In addition to this, quoting Austin, he makes a deep analysis about the ruling aspect of the moral character or «international courtesy», which may not impose real but ethical sanctions, as we have recently observed in the UN crisis on the US-Iraq conflict.

The author's analysis turns out very consistent with the new times, as if it the capacity is to impose sanctions using mainly the strength, it would be assimilated to the sanction putting the ethical and moral principles aside. This analysis arise the inevitable necessity of a world international society, otherwise the most powerful causes would legitimate themselves, instead of Law.

It is important to point out that the inclusion made by the author about those aspects, reveal his discomfort regarding the current topics of International Law. He concludes quoting Brotons (1997) and states that the institutional lacking of the international society empowers the role splitting of its members. It means that the States by acting on its own, also act by the international society. The author ends stating that the aforementioned quote is also assumed by affirming that the most powerful States, using international hypocrisy, are capable of invoking the splitting of its members.

Another aspect analyzed by the intellectual lawyer, Luis Manuel Marcano Salazar, in this specific matter is related to the efficacy of International Law, in which it is deeply reviewed 3 existing items on the concept: provisions, consent and self-decision-making power. Afterwards, the author focuses on the analysis of the legal nature of International Public Law, starting with the idea that each State's Constitution is the legitimate logical ground that backs up Public International Law. At this point he begins the extensive analysis of the «Venezuelan legal ground[1]».

Chapter V is referred to the International Community and the author innovates by systematically analyzing this topic, which refers to the aforesaid Community during the XXI century, adding the «hegemonic global State» concept and some interesting considerations regarding the beginning of the century. The author also incorporates the war against terrorism, which started after September 11th 2001, as well as the war in Iraq, which ended with the defeating of Saddam Hussein.

On this matter, the author incorporates his intensely analysis about region-States and nucleon-States, as an extension of the power due to national security reasons. It is also incorporated the problem of war in the new world order and the diverse author's conceptions, such as Fukuyama (1992), Huntington (1997), Morgenthau (1963), Kennan (1952) and others, who consider the conflict begins because of cultural differences or the interest/power relation. So, the author approaches himself to the global war concept and humanitarian reasons interventions, throughout which the regional-continental area is breached, settling the breaking points of conflicts and the war against terrorism.

---

1 Quoting the content of article 152 of the Constitution of the Bolivarian Republic of Venezuela and the different acts referring to international provisions, such as the Criminal Code, the Civil Procedural Code and the Approbatory Law of the American Convention on Human Rights, besides noting the Pact of San José, Costa Rica, as well as the Inter-American Democratic Charter.

Another important distinction analyzed by the author relies on the difference between international society and international community. In the final part he analyses the western European world. From that point on he goes deeper regarding the UN and OAS structures, and finalizes the chapter with the ethnological conception of Islamic Law. Also, he briefly refers to the new unipolar or multipolar world.

The author stays apart from the Eurocentric aspect of International Law and its Greek-Roman heritage with Christianity sustenance. The expansion of Islam and its integrated legislation -in which both political and religious power are mixed-, its dominant spirit in the past and demographic reality are valid reasons so that Islamism -with political expression in the States and the International System- be considered nowadays. So far, 56 governments claim themselves as Muslim ones and over 1.300 million of human beings believe in the Coram. As International Law conceptions have brought confrontations due to the conflict with civilizations, a synthesis must be addressed, as it has been the recent creation of the International Criminal Court.

Chapter VI is dedicated to analyze the Foreign Policy and its relation with International Public Law. Its study is systematically approached until the Venezuelan Foreign Policy is explored, and quotes some important Venezuelan authors such as Elsa Cardozo Da Silva, Carlos Romero and Maria Teresa Romero. Finally, the author is mainly focused on the connection of Public International Law with International Relations, as well as the political system.

It is important to point out that the masterpiece written by this young intellectual man who is an expert in the grounds of Law, Politics, History and Diplomacy, represents an important contribution to the studies of International Law, professors and students, as well as to those interested in the diplomatic field. It is a creative example the work done by Luis Manuel Marcano Salazar, in terms of how International Public aspects are suggested. He goes further of the simple rule to explore an interdisciplinary world that analyses the event from different perspectives, based on a wide bibliography that allows valuing the dedication and perseverance of the author.

Caracas, September 2019.
JULIO CESAR PINEDA
Ambassador
International Legal and Political Analyst.

PRELIMINARY NOTE

Public International Law is an evolving discipline, due to the transformations that daily occur in human thought and International System, and continuous changes are required to be observed slowly, meticulously and responsibly. Because of the fact that it is considered and conventional discipline derived from the initiative of subject of law and due to the lack of a centralized jurisdictional body, its complex study becomes more unpredictable every day. An International legal phenomenon could provide political, economic, sociological and geographical consequences that need a solid knowledge of its origins, the concepts, definitions, principles and regulations. It is a connecting dynamic among Public International Law with Politics, History, International Relations, Sociology, Geography and other disciplines that explain more easily certain complex phenomena in a constant turbulent world.

It is not easy for an entry-level College student to get to know and understand the latest events if they don't have a basic theorist background that may constitute an instrument for that matter. The enormous amount of bibliography of this subject existing in book stores is part of a contribution to its studies, headed to different areas: one which is very knowledgeable of the discipline as analysts, researchers and professors; the other one is composed of students starting or finishing his college education.

When we talk about Fundamentals of Public International Law, we head our attention to the latter area, with great importance, since it is the moment in which the pupil may consolidate a conceptual background wide enough to be academically developed. An international jurisdictional decision or a treaty can be both interpreted, and even a case can be analyzed if the conceptual foundations and principles from where they are derived are known. The present masterpiece attempts to contribute with this initial education when we study the concepts, principles and history of Public International Law in every chapter, and also how it has developed in this changing world. Nonetheless, the amendments made in the new Foreign Service Law allow undergraduate professionals from other disciplines not related to Public International Law and International Relations, to apply for Public Examination Entrance to enter the diplomatic career. This masterpiece is also headed to those professionals.

It is not expected to innovate about areas that have been quite analyzed by Venezuelan and foreign specialists. We aim for facilitating and comprehending the study of the discipline in an educational and organized manner. Our contribution attempts to be a basic and necessary instrument for the student, and also a bedside book to those who wish to learn about the topic.

LUIS M. MARCANO SALAZAR

CHAPTER I

PUBLIC INTERNATIONAL LAW

Definition. The object of Public International Law. Denominations. Divisions. Historic evolutions. Public International Law as Universal Law. Interactions and differences with the Domestic Law: dualism and monism. Interactions with other sciences: international politics and international ethics.

«Law is the art of the good and the just»

Celsus

Definition

The study of Public International Law has led to a revision of the bibliographic diversity mostly produced in the past twentieth century. As a result, there are a series of definitions we find worth analyzing in order to come up with one concept that caters to today's reality. According to Antonio Truyol, the Public International Law «may be defined as a set of laws that rules the relations amongst States» (1977:7). Alejandro Rodriguez Carrion defines them as «the set of laws that rule the international society and its members in the prosecution of individual and collective social interests» (1998:88).

Gaviria Lievano says that it is a «predominantly legal science (...), which doesn't mean that it may be considered an autonomous and independent science» (1998:2). Alberto Vega Molano delimits it as a «set of laws that rule the relations amongst international subjects» (1995: 17-18). Marco Monroy Cabra defines it as «the branch of the Public Law that (...)studies the relations amongst the States and other subjects of the International Law, as well as the organization and operations of the international community» (1998:3). Cesareo Gutierrez Espada believes that the Public International Law «is the result of treaties and customs that derive from the States» (1995:33).

Georg Schwarzenberger has a less positivist approach. He says that «a society in which the power is the main consideration, the main aim of the Law is to help maintain the predominance of the force and the hierarchy based on the power and to give this system the respectability and sanction derived from the establishment of the law» (1960:176). Adolfo Miaja de la Muela admits that, due to its nature, International Law «is not limited to ruling the relations amongst States, but it also norms the relations amongst the International Organizations, the States and other entities that hold individuals accountable for duties and entitled to rights (1974:32). This asseveration coincides with Henri Rolin's (1950). Antonio Linares says the Public International Law «is firmly practiced in the international relations (which makes it) compulsory» (1992:11).

Julio Diena (1941) comes up with a double meaning for Public International Law:

> ...it may be considered science and Positive Law. The first one may be defined as the science that focuses its object of study on the legal principles aimed to rule the relations amongst the members of the International Legal Community; The second one may be defined (...) as the set of rules that States and other entities that are part of the International Legal Community are willing to abide to in the course of their relations (p. 2).

Manuel Diez de Velasco says that the set of rules that contain the Public International Law is conceived as the «International legal system» (1973:51). The Portuguese author Paul Reuter (1981) says the Public International Law rules the relations amongst sovereign States.

A classic study by Max Sorensen states that the denomination «International Law» (1973:51) is «strictly technical as it names a legal system that primarily aims to rule the relations amongst States» (1958:53). The Venezuelan authors Daniel Guerra Iñiguez (1985:7) and Fermin Toro Jimenez (2001:16) agree on defining Public international Law as the «set of laws that rule the relations amongst the subjects of Public International Law».

The different definitions brought up here[2] allow proposing a new definition of our own, taking four variables into consideration:

1. International structure
2. Subjects and role players in the international community
3. Processes that have an impact and affect or even direct the relations amongst the national States and international organizations.
4. The principle of sovereign equality[3]

---

[2] Beside the one we presented in our piece Introduction to the study of International Relations: a theoretical approach to foreign policy and Public International Law.

[3] Which we will deal with in other topic related to the U.N. Resolution 2625.

We define Public International Law as the set of conventional, compulsory laws that are influenced by the international structure and its processes and rules the relations amongst the sovereign States and other subjects. These do not require international acknowledgement by the nations because they do play a role at an international level, as done by the individual and Non-governmental Organizations.

OBJECT OF THE PUBLIC INTERNATIONAL LAW

By studying the diverse definitions of the Public International Law proposed by different authors and revising our definition based on the transformations of the international structure, we may conclude that the object of the Public International Law is dichotomous; that is to say, it entails double purpose. As a science, it studies the legal, historical, social and economic principles that have an influence on the very existence of international conventions in order to explain the legal phenomena from an epistemological point of view. As a subject, it provides the basis for ruling the international community in order to ensure any controversies arisen amongst the States or other legal subjects are properly dealt with within the boundaries of international justice.

Despite the bibliographic impact factor that affects this definition and in light of its lack of originality as a result of a reflection of what has been written on the subject, we believe it plausible to approach the Public International Law as an indivisible entirety; that is to say, it is science and subject, which means it both analyzes the «legal principles» and rules the States and subjects in order to guarantee the empire of the international law, to solve issues or simply to explain legal international phenomena, such as the acknowledgement of States and governments, which defines it as a unilateral act of law as well as the result of a rational decision derived by mostly political interests.

DENOMINATIONS

There have been different denominations that indicate the names that Public International Law has received throughout its history. Notice it has not always been the same subject because it has been modified in time. The oldest denomination of the Public International Law can be found in Asia, where the Indian treaties of law known as *Drama-Sastras* had the power to rule religious, ethics, political, legal and other affairs of the sovereign State (Stadmuller, 1961:10).

The Hellenics gave the name of *presbeis* to the Law of ambassadors and *kerykes* to the Law of consuls (Ibid.:24). In Roman times, Public International Law was known as *Ius Fetiale*, due to the international nature the *fetial* priests had developed (Diena, 1941). Years later, the Romans named it *Ius Gentium* or people's law, or the law common to all peoples, according to Ulpianus - the nations (Truyol, 1995: 22). Francisco Vitoria named it «Quod naturalis ratio inter omnes gentes constituit, vocatur jus gentium»[4]. Ricardo Zouch used the denomination «Juris inter gentes explicatio»[5] for the piece that versed on Public International Law. Contemporarily, Jeremy Bentham[6] used the name that more closely matches the one we use today: *International Law;* which was followed by the French denomination *Droit International,* and the Italian one *Diritto Internationale;* by Vitoria and Zouch (Diena, 1941: 2-3).

DIVISIONS

Finding a practical and useful division of the Public International Law in the current available legal doctrine is more than a mere data collection task: it is a rational and intellectual job. Therefore, we will not take any doctrinal position and will present our proposal which suggests Public International Law can be divided into three categories: according to its object of regulation, to its nature and to its purposes.

- If based on its object of regulation, it can be divided into *General Public International Law*: it studies the relations amongst States and subject of International Law; and *Special Public International Law*: it analyzes and explains the treaties and unilateral acts of law.
- If based on its nature, it can be divided into *Ideal Public International Law*: it studies justice and ethics inherent in the relations across the international community; and *Positivist Public International Law*: it studies the set of rules and laws that can actually be effective in the international community.
- If based on its purposes, it can be divided into *Procedural Public International Law*: it studies the procedures that States follow when engaged in contentious relationships with other States, as well as the procedures followed by international bodies and legal instances in the international community (such as the International Court in The Hague or the Nuremberg Court); and Methodological Public International Law: It is produced by the international treatise writers in order to find new approaches that reformulate the legal aspects in the international academic discussion.

HISTORIC EVOLUTION AND CHARACTERISTICS

Why is it important to revise and study the past? To better interpret the present? We do it to understand the evolution and development of the human

---

4 «That the natural reasoning gives to the men to constitute a Law amongst peoples» originally translated from Latin to Spanish by the writer of this book.

5 «Explanation of the Law amongst peoples» originally translated from Latin to Spanish by the writer of this book.

6 English Philosopher.

being in the society and the institutions with the aim of finding an explanation of the past, based on present events. This is why rediscovering Public International Law presents an intellectual exercise that is closely linked to the definition of History. In his piece *What is History* (1961), Edward H. Carr discards the theory of objective History; He actually suggests that an author's explanation is the historical data per se. We will take this approach to analyze the evolution of the Public International Law based on the contributions by Frederic Pearson and Martin Rochester (2000) about the periods the international system has faced. It is important to note that our approach is western-influenced, despite our efforts to keep ourselves objective.

Ancient times

The most primitive reference we have about the existence of a Public International Law can be found it the pre-State times. We name it so as the legal and jurisprudential protection as well as the execution of the law was not exclusively managed by the Public Powers of the administration of a State Justice (Stadmuller, 1961). In the pre-State times, the society was organized in tribes and a Private Self-execution Law was applied - blood revenge, application of divine justice. This didn't only happen in non-European peoples, but also in Germanic ones, the primitive Greek societies and in the legal relations of the old Israel. However, the pre-State society had its own conception of the legal matters, which manifested itself in the protection of the naked, the right to asylum and the immunity of the foreign treaties. The Talion law was exercised: «eye for an eye».

Nonetheless, based on the documents available from those times, there was no international body consolidated. The war dominated the lives of the different tribes permanently. The territory of the neighbor was considered an enemy land; therefore, the mission of sacking was considered a heroic act. The prisoner was deprived of the subjective right and was converted into a slave or even killed (Ibid).

The bibliography available shows that the oldest international treaty took place in Mesopotamia, towards the end of the year 3010 B.C. (Truyol, 1995). It was a treaty between Ennanatum, king of Lagash and the city of Umma. It was written in Sumerian and it contains the acknowledgement Umma made of the new boundary. It also contained a divine sanction (Ibid:19). Additionally, the first treaty discovered in its original form was made between the king of Elba and the sovereign of Assyria (Ibid). Such treaty celebrated the relations of friendship and commerce in place between the two kingdoms. We can also find the treaty between the king of Akkad, Naram-Sin and the king of Elam.

The Greeks had an equalitarian relation with the Persian Empire, Cartago and Rome. The impact of the ethnicity, the linguistics, the religion and culture over the law derived from the feeling they had about belonging to a differentiated community, despite the political atomization in which the City-States were involved. This resulted in relations that were ruled by consecutive and conventional norms with a structure that differentiates from the definition we currently know of international norms. However, a sort of International Intra-Hellenic law existed and was based on common practice sanctioned by the religion. Diplomatic communication was common amongst cities and the emissaries (diplomats) had clear, well established, open relationships. This was also the case in Rome.

The international Hellenic Law manifested itself through the link amongst the cities. There was also a very strict War Law in which there were no humanitarian concessions for the prisoners and the peace was ruled through a short-term pact. More norms were later created in order to mitigate the effects of the war. On the other hand, the Hellenic Stoic Philosophy allowed putting together a set of ethical and legal principles all men regardless had to abide to.

In the case of Rome, it was the Domestic Law the one that enabled the construction of an International Law. As previously mentioned, the *fetial* priests, whose opinion was crucial to make a decision on starting a war, put an end to peace or claim damages caused to Rome, represented a sacred law known as *Ius Fetiale*, which was later replaced by the *Ius Gentium*. People's Law filled the legal gap for dealing with foreign peoples. Due to such absence, foreigners lacked a law and it was believed Civil Law could not be applied to them. This enabled People's Law to become stronger as trade with foreign places became more complicated, so such law allowed to rule the relations with non-Roman peoples. This is why we believe the internal Roman Law set the foundation for International Law. People's Law gradually differentiated from Civil Law because it was more flexible in the construction of norms that ruled the daily practice in the all men's common needs. This meant *Ius Gentium* became some sort of Universal Private Law that later saw the incorporation of the institutions of the Public Law (Ibid).

In Iran, The Arsacid Empire had reigned, later followed by the Sananid Empire. The Romans had no choice but to co-exist with them. In this case, treaties were agreed with clauses related to the continental trade, the freedom of cult for Christians in the Persian Empire and a rigorous treatment to prisoners which contrasted with the one given to refugees (Ibid.:30).

In the middle-age Christian western, the Germanic peoples resulted in independent kingdoms: The Franc in Gallia (France), the Visigoth in Spain, the Ostrogoth and the Lombard in Italy, The Anglo, Just and the Saxon in England and the Vandal in Africa. This resulted in an implicit territorial agreement manifested in relations that were later established, yet with the same violence present during war. The most important characteristics of this middle age-Christian Law were:

- An effort of the church to minimize the fights.
- Feudal or private wars were prohibited.
- The military activity was dominated by the principle of gentleness based on a code of honor.
- The theologists demanded that the public war between two kingdoms be subject to certain conditions.
- Arbitration was commonly consulted, and the Pope was a very important instance.
- The Law of the treaties was reinforced by the custom and oath or tokens and hostages

The International Law in the middle-age muslim world, specifically its People's Law, had an imperial-Theocratic structure that explains the problems in the relationships with what they called the infidel. Many intellectual thinkers focused on the international relations within their systems from a philosophic point of view. At that pre-State stage, the Natural Law had predominance over the Positivist Law because the agreements between peoples were sanctioned by the divinity, which was expressed in their kings and emperors.

The international classic system (1648 - 1789)

According to the periodical order suggested by Pearson and Rochester (2000:38), the classic system started in 1648 with the Peace of Westphalia, which put an end to the Thirty Years' War. The national States that appeared in this period all had the same characteristics: Central and sovereign government, settled population and a well-defined territory. The Peace of Westphalia, contained in the Osnabruck and Monster treaties, has been the base of the European Public Law (*Ius publicum Europeaum*), also known as the European People's Law. This also allowed establishing equality between the Catholicism and Lutheranism at an international level.

As per this period, the principle of balance between forces is acknowledged and reproduced in article II of the treaty of peace between Great Britain and Spain, which was agreed in Utrecht on July 13th 1713. One of the main characteristics of the European People's Law was the generalization of the permanent diplomatic representations since the XVI century (Truyol, 1995). However, this principle did not guarantee a stable international order because its practice was made easier by the dynastic solidarities.

The number of subjects of People's Law after the Peace of Westphalia caused inequalities to be visible enough as to be ignored in the exercise of the diplomacy, despite equality was claimed by the sovereignty. Besides, the oath to confirm the treaties began to disappear, but the divine intervention was still present (Ibid.:76).

After Utrecht, Trade treaties were as important as peace treaties. The treaty of Methuen[7] between Great Britain and Portugal was very important for bilateral relations. Such treaty contained Portugal's acceptance to the introduction of English wools, which were subject to a tax of 23% in exchange for the reduction of the Customs rights for Portuguese wines in England. A treaty from the period in question worth mentioning is the one signed by Great Britain and France in 1786, which included the clause of most privileged nation. There were also many treaties on slavery between 1713 and 1789.

The characteristics of this period can be summarized as follows:

- Religious equality
- Relative equality across the States
- The establishment of permanent diplomatic missions
- The application of the principle of the right to self-determination
- The use of French as a diplomatic language
- The condition that enables States to develop international relations that are not subordinated to the pontificate
- The ratification of the principle of Divine Law of the Kings

From a doctrinal point of view, a deep intellectualism in the treatise writers from the period in question is vastly documented across the bibliography available. Marco Monroy Cabra cites Cesar Sepulveda saying that «it had been believed that the doctrine of the Public International Law had been born with the dutch writer Huig De Groot in the XVIII century» (1998:55). However, The theological Spanish lawyers from centuries XVI and XVII were the ones who brought the Public International Law to light. For example, Francisco de Vitoria was a key figure in the Spanish ius natural approach. There also were positivists such as Ricardo Zouch, Cornelius Van Bynkershoek, Emeterio de Batel, Juan Jacobo Moser and Jorge Federico Von Martens.

The transitional international system (1789 - 1945)

It is important to note that most of the treatise writers agree on identifying a period that goes from 1919 to 1945, which began right after the end of I World War. However, we believe that due to the characteristics of a transitional period, we should stick to the aforementioned lapse, the reason being the tendency to use the force as an instrument of foreign policy did not finish with the end of I World War, but with the end of the II World War. Hence, we suggest a transitional period beginning with the French Revolution in of 1789 and finishing with the end of II World War in 1945.

---

7 Named by British negotiator Lord John Methuen.

Jeremy Bentham published «A plan for a universal and perpetual peace» as part of his essays of his piece «Principles of International Law» (1780) (Rodriguez, 1998: 87). He acknowledges the principle of advertising, which means the end of secret diplomacy and the demand for a free press and freedom of information. Additionally, he holds the need of codifying the International Law and suggests the inclusion of the following aspects in the Public International Law:

- The need for an urgent disarmament
- The prohibition of alliances for attacks
- The creation of an arbitration court
- The freedom of trade
- The end of colonialism

It is important to note that while Bentham was writing this doctrine, another key event took place in 1789: The independence of the United States of America. The answer to the question of whether there was a connection amongst all of the events taking place then is a solid yes. It was the result of the influence of liberalism in the western world. Norm-wise speaking, this was reflected in a key document from that time: «the Declaration of the Rights of the Man and of the Citizen», as a result of the French Revolution. Another important fact from the period in question was the Congress of Vienna in 1815.

The end of the Napoleonic wars was sealed in the Treaty of Paris on May 30th, 1814. Article 32 of such treaty stipulated that a general congress of all belligerent powers had to be called for in order to complete its content. Later, on November 20th, 1815, a treaty in Paris that modified some norms on the previous treaty was signed after the congress had finished. Another important event took place in the same year: the Congress of Vienna, which aimed to set a more stable environment in Europe through the establishment of peace for a century.

On the other hand, the final document of the congress set the foundation for the development of an International fluvial law, stipulating the freedom for sailing the rivers that crossed or separated different States. The Congress of Vienna also wrote a declaration of the powers, which versed on the abolishment of black slavery, which they thought was a humiliation against the principles of humanity and universal ethics.

The spirit of the Congress of Vienna was led by the principle of legitimacy and was founded by the return of the monarchy to France. The defenders of such principle justified the right of intervention on its behalf, in the service of the restoration of the threatened order. Nevertheless, its artificial nature acted against it: it didn't respond to the needs of the people because they were not part. Sovereignty lied in the king. Yet, this changed due to the impact caused by the revolutions in France and the United States, in which popular sovereignty was transitionally established.

The policy of intervention became part of a system and received further support when the United Kingdom and France joined it after the treaty of Aquisgran in 1818. This is how the Pentarchy was created. A new revolution burst out in France in 1848, after a short republican period, and in 1852 Louis Napoleon proclaimed himself emperor, opposing the stipulations of the Treaty of Vienna. Napoleon III managed to arrange an alliance with England in order to support Turkey in its war against Russia. That is how the Crimean War started, which ended with the Congress of Paris in 1856.

From that year on, the environment to encourage the growth of feelings of nationalism increased after the creation of national States (Belgium in 1831 and Greece in 1832). Later, the European provinces dominated by the Ottoman Empire managed to defeat the Turkish domination after the Balkan wars in 1912 and 1913, which resulted in a new State known as Albania.

This process enabled a very noticeable development of a Positivist Public International Law. Not only did many western States abided to it but also eastern ones such as Turkey and Japan. The beginning of the I World War in 1914 was the framework for a series of changes in International Law matters. They will be studied further in this book, which is why it is important to revise the historical and political variables that had an effect on the beginning of the aforementioned global conflict.

I World War (1914 - 1918)

I World War started on 28 July 1914 as a conflict between the Austrian-Hungarian Empire and Serbia. However, it later developed into an armed conflict across Europe when the declaration of war by Austria-Hungary extended to Russia on August 1st 1914 and it then resulted in a world war in which 32 countries participated. This war ended in 1918. 28 out of the countries that participated, in which Great Britain, France, Serbia, Russia, Italy and the United States were part of, fought against the coalition formed by the central empires: Germany, Austria-Hungary, the Ottoman Empire and Bulgaria.

The most immediate cause of the hostilities between Austria-Hungary and Serbia was the murder of the Archduke Franz Ferdinand from Habsburg, heir to the Austrian-Hungarian throne. This event took place in Sarajevo (Bosnia)[8] on June 28th 1914. The murder was committed by the Serbian nationalist Gavrilo Princip. However, there are deeper causes of the conflict

8 This was part of the Austrian-Hungarian Empire by then; Bosnia-Herzegovina today.

that can be traced back to the European history of the XIX century, more specifically the economic and political tendencies that dominated Europe since 1871, the year in which the II German Empire was founded and emerged as a power. The real causes of the I World War were the intense nationalist spirit that spread across Europe throughout the XIX century and the beginning of the XX century; the economic and political rivalry amongst different nations and the process of militarization and armament that was typical in the international society in the last third of the XIX century, starting with the creation of alliances in conflict. Why did that happen?

The French Revolution and the Napoleonic wars had disseminated the idea of democracy all across Europe. Hence, the idea of peoples that shared the same ethnic background, the same tongue and the same political ideas had the right to form independent States. Nonetheless, the lack of a principle of national self-determination resulted in dynastic and reactive forces deciding the destiny of European affairs in the Congress of Vienna in 1815. Many of the peoples that wished to be autonomous remained subdue to local dynasties or to other nations.

The German States, which were integrated by the Germanic Confederation, were divided in different dukedoms, principalities and kingdoms. Italy was divided into different political units and some of them were under foreign control; the French and the Flemish Belgians from the Netherlands were controlled by the Dutch. The revolutions and the strong nationalist movements in the XIX century managed to avoid many of the impositions that were going to be agreed on Vienna. An example is Belgium, which obtained the independence from the Netherlands in 1830. Yet, other nationalist conflicts in other areas of Europe were still unsolved in the early XX century, which caused strong tension in the regions involved and amongst different European nations. One of the most important nationalist movements, the Pan slavism, played a key role in the events that preceded the war.

The nationalist spirit was also visible in the economic matters. The Industrial Revolution, which began in Great Britain in the late XVIII century, in France in the early XIX century and in Germany after the year 1870, caused an increase of manufactured goods, which led these countries to look for foreign markets where the products could be placed, which created the need for a series of legal changes in the international scenario. This enriched the conception and use of the International Law.

The area in which the expansion policy led by Europe was mostly developed was Africa, where the colonial interests faced conflicts frequently. The economic rivalry for the domination of the African territory amongst France, Great Britain and Germany almost resulted in a European war between 1898 and 1914.

The end of the I World War was sealed with the Conference of Paris in 1919-1920. This event produced the treaties that legally determined the end of the war with different adversaries. The first and best known is the Treaty of Versailles, on June 28th, 1919, with Germany. Other treaties were agreed were the Treaty of Saint-Germain, with Austria; the Treaty of Neilly, with Bulgaria; The Treaty of Trianon, with Hungary; and the Treaty of Sevres, with Turkey. The most important challenge for the winning countries was the creation of the League of Nations. This idea came from one of the fourteen points the president of the United States, Woodrow Wilson, had presented to the Congress on January 8th, 1818. This point aimed to inspire the future peace. However, the failure of the League of Nations was crudely evident when the world became engaged in another world war.

The II World War (1939 - 1945)

The II World War had a background: France, United Kingdom and the United States had achieved the objectives in the conflict that started in 1914. They managed to have Germany limit its military potential at certain degree and reorganized Europe and the world according to their interests. However, the political disagreements between France and the United Kingdom in the interwar period (1919 - 1939) were frequent and both countries did not trust their capacity for keeping the peace. On the other hand, the United States, disappointed by its European counterparts that did not pay the debt resulted from the war, began an isolationist policy.

There were different attempts to achieve a long-lasting piece in the 20s. Firstly, the League of Nations was created in 1920 as an arbitration entity in which countries could deal with their differences. The powers of this society were limited to the persuasion and different degrees of ethical and economic sanctions that members could comply with or not.

The main international powers agreed on limiting the number of war ships to a specific amount in the Conference of Washington (1921 - 1922). The treaties of Locarno, which were signed in this Swiss city in a conference that was held in 1925, guaranteed the frontiers between France and Germany and included an arbitration agreement between Germany and Poland. 63 nations signed a Treaty to outlaw war known as the Pact of Paris or Pact Briand-Kellog, in which countersigners agreed on giving up on war as an instrument of their national policies and committed to resolve all their international conflict using peaceful means. The countries involved had previously decided not to include the self-defense wars in this attempt to outlaw war.

One of the objectives of the winners of the I World War had been to ensure the world would become a safe place for democracy. The post-war German republic (also known as the Republic of Weimar) adopted a democratic constitution, like many other States that were created or re-created during or after the conflict. However, a series of movements in the 20s spread across

Europe disseminating an extreme, military-based nationalism known as «fascism», word originated from the Italian. This movement came up as a more efficient alternative than democracy to satisfy people's needs and it also portrayed itself as a safe defense against communism. Benito Mussolini started the first fascist dictatorship in Italy in 1922.

Adolf Hitler promised to abandon the Treaty of Versailles and find more vital space for the German people, a right he thought they deserved because they belonged to a superior race. The Great Depression, which began in the early 30s affected Germany strongly. The moderated parties could not achieve an agreement on the possible solutions and a great deal of citizens decided to trust the Nazis. Hitler was named Chancellor of Germany in 1933 and then emerged as a dictator after a series of political maneuvers.

Hitler expressed his disagreement with the clauses related to the military imposed to Germany in the Treaty of Versailles. He organized a new Army, resumed the military service and he even had the chance to test some weapons he had acquired during the Spanish Civil War (1936-1939). He participated in the aforementioned war supporting the rebel military agents, together with the Italian troops of Mussolini, who decided to support them after they conquered Ethiopia (1935 - 1936) through a brief armed conflict. The treaties signed by Germany, Italy and Japan - beside other countries such as Hungary, Romania and Bulgaria - since 1936 - the year in which Germany and Italy signed their first treaty - to 1941, resulted in the creation of the Axis Alliance: Rome-Berlin-Tokyo.

The War that extended from 1939 to 1945 raised a new concept of the Public International Law when some leaders of the National Socialist Party were sentenced to death for crimes against the humanity and genocide in the Nuremberg court. Similarly, there were courts that judged Japanese military officers for crimes against the humanity.

The system that followed the II World War

The end of II World War produced the reorganization of the international system. The creation of the United Nations (UN) called the whole planet to a world of peace. However, the period that followed the end of II World War was marked by the bipolarity East-West in which two countries became the protagonists: The United States and the Union of Soviet Socialist Republics. The Cold War defines the conflict these two countries silently held. At a lesser scale, there were different conflicts: The Korean war, the missile crisis in 1962, Vietnam, Angola and Central America. The main characteristic was the ideological conflict between the right-wing democracies and the left-wing governments.

A very significant fact for the Public International Law was the end of the Cold War, which resulted in an unstable, unipolar world, with frequent interventions of the most powerful countries on the UN's behalf. Different courts to judge crimes against humanity were created as well as courts to judge genocide, war crimes in Rwanda, Yugoslavia and Sierra Leone, and a Court with international jurisdiction to judge atrocities: The International Criminal Court.

The system after September 11th, 2001

One of the most important characteristics of this period was the recrudescence of the international terrorism, which has put the world on a new conflictive scenario, with unknown consequences so far. We should note that, from our point of view, the Public International Law has not been very useful to stop the violence that has arisen, especially when the United States, in its role as a powerful country, attempts to impose its hegemony on weaker States.

It is important to note that an extensive bibliographic production has fed the studies of Public International Law. Some of the most important authors are Alfred Vedross (1967), Hans Kelsen (1994), Barcia Trelles (1948), etc. Some Venezuelan authors that deserve credit are Fermin Toro Jimenez (2001) and Daniel Guerra Iñiguez (1985), whose production should be considered important for the study of contemporary Public International Law.

American International Law

The American International Law was first seen in the diplomatic documents resulted from the Congress of Panama. The eighth clause of the Act of 1834, which was issued by the Mexican government to get another congress together, stipulated that one of the objectives of the meeting was to set the foundation of the Public Law that would rule the relations amongst the new republics. However, as explained by Luis Fernando Alvarez Londono, we believe that the American International Law is a set of rules that aim to rule problems and situations that typically happen in the States of America (1998).

Public International Law as Universal Law

Public International Law is the result of the bilateral or multilateral conventions or unilateral actions performed by the States or subject of law in the context of international relations. This condition enables it to have principles with a legal nature that may be applied universally. Guerra Iniguez (1985: 37) believes that the universality of the Public International Law may be explained by the condition of the States to be part of an international community.

We believe that the concept of International Law as Universal Law is produced in response to the limiting categories that place it in a determined region: European International Law, American International Law, etc. However, as opposed to the opinion of the respectable jurist Guerra Iniguez, we believe that the conception of Public International Law as Universal Law may not be applicable in a world governed by the hegemony of the powerful countries that justify the use of the force over the balance of the international norms.

Relations and differences with the Domestic Law: dualism and monism

The Public International Law as a ruling body may be differentiated from the Domestic Law mainly due to its source. While the Positivist Domestic Law is sanctioned by a legislative entity, the International Law is the product of agreements amongst subject of International Law or acts of law. The Domestic Law is codified in acts and laws; The Public International Law is found in explicit or implicit agreements amongst States and other subjects of International Law.

Theories in both disciplines have been proposed to explain the relation between them. These theories are known as the dualism and monism. Treatise writers consider this discussion has been overcome because there is consensus in considering both disciplines as separate and different and none of them is subordinated to the other; however, for those who begin studies in international law matters, it is important to revise the theoretic proposals.

Dualist theory

This theory suggests International Law and Domestic Law are two completely different systems (Truyol 1977:110) that do not hold subordinating relations of any kind (Monroy Cabra, 1998). The dualist theory was sustained by Triepel and Anzilotti (Antokoletz, 1938: 58). Their premise was the source of Public International Law is the common will of two or more States, while the source of Domestic Law was the willingness derived from a legislative body.

Alberto Vergara Molano finds three types of differences: field of application, sources and subjects (1995: 28). When referred to the field of application, there is a prevalence of the legal rules over the relations amongst States and other subjects of International Law, while the Domestic Law is valid for a given State and its population. When referred to its sources, the International Law results from the willingness of two or more subjects of International Law, while the Domestic Law results from the power of a legislative body. When referred to the subject, the International Law is valid for States and other subjects of law on a reciprocal basis, while the Domestic Law is only applicable to the individuals only.

The theory in question suggests both Laws have a diversity of sources and subjects; hence, there is no conflict amongst them. The dualist theory 'emancipates' the International Law from the Domestic Law because the first one acknowledges the willingness of the States being controlled and the second one is the willingness of only one State. This statement agrees with Antonio Linares's words: «The International Law and the Domestic Law belong to autonomous legal rules» (1992: 31). This means that in order to make a Public International Law norm and which is acknowledged by the legal system of a determined country, a sovereign act of State from a legislative body is required.

Monist Theory

This theory was sustained by Hans Kelsen (1994), Duguit (1926) and Krabbe (1906) and it suggests that the Law is only one and may not be separated because it is not the result of the will of a State or an individual but «something superior»[9]; that is to say, a norm that creates a unique legal system. This is why there may be no conflicts between the International and the Domestic Laws. Vergara Molano cites Hans Kelsen and says that «this doctrine was based on the unity of the sets of legal norms» (1995: 29).

Unlike the dualist theory, the monist theory is explained by a ruling subordination. Some consider there are two monist theories: one sustains the International Law is subordinated to the Domestic Law (nationalists) and the other hierarchizes the International Law over the Domestic Law because a superior ruling system derives from it.

Kelsen sustained his theory on the positivist scientific approach which took the Law as an indivisible unit and made it its object of study. Scelle considered there was a delegating relation between the International Law and the Domestic Law (Truyol 1977: 112).

RELATIONS WITH OTHER SCIENCES; INTERNATIONAL POLITICS AND INTERNATIONAL ETHICS

The Public International Law does not only relate to International Politics and International Ethics. It has more extensive relations with other sciences because it makes use of History, Sociology, Communication, Information Science, Politics and Diplomacy, amongst others. The relation between the foundation of the Public International Law and International Politics and Ethics are explained by an axiomatic and dichotomist conception. The interests and means of negotiation should be observed for the application of the rules that are object of regulation in International Politics. International Ethics ensures compliance with ethical and ontological principles.

International Politics are composed by a set of actions that enable the governments to manage their foreign relations and they are ruled by ends, goals, targets and results. The State aims to achieve the pursued objectives through it without regards to the methods used for the protection of national interests and therefore using the power available. The Law is an instrument of politics.

On the other hand, International Ethics is manifested in a set of values that overcome the legal nature that rules the States. They are provisions subscribed by the United Nations and other international organizations such as the prohibition to people trafficking and the use of drugs (Gaviria Lievano, 1998).

---

[9] Jusnaturalistic approach.

CHAPTER II

FOUNDATION AND SOURCES OF THE PUBLIC INTERNATIONAL LAW

Foundation and different schools. Classification of the sources. The treaties. Other sources of Public International Law.

«Every law has been made because of the men»

Hermogenianus

FOUNDATION AND DIFFERENT SCHOOLS

As appointed by Guerra Iniguez, the foundation of the Public International Law is «the legal basis for the International Law and becomes the rationale of its very existence» (1985:26-27). Yet, it is important to note that the State is the responsible to legitimate the obligation derived from the Public International Law as a response to the absence of an international legislative body.

On a different matter, the concept of 'source' refers to origin or the place where something is derived from. In its Purest Theory of the Law (1994), Kelsen thought the word had four different meanings: the validity of the rules, its creation per se, its manifestation and the principles that rule it.

When studying Public International Law, it is necessary to consider the possible contribution these meanings may give to its study. However, before we begin to explore this topic, it is worth revising the different schools that provide the foundation to the Public International Law, according to the approach authors such as Guerra Iniguez, Alvarez Londono, Monroy Cabra amongst others, have suggested.

- Theological School: It believes in a religious foundation for the Public International Law, which is why the law is subordinated to the definition of ethics and religion.
- Roman School: It suggests that the Ius Gentium, as referred to in Chapter I, is the foundation of the Public International Law because

it deals with rules that were applicable to peoples or nations beyond the frontiers of the Empire.

- Ius-naturalistic School: It believes in the existence of an applicable Law to all men, to whom a «natural reason» provided with a perpetual right derived from God.
- Positivist School: it suggests that the Public International Law is founded on the treaties, conventions and the custom, as a result of the collective will of the nations.
- Voluntaristic theory: it is derived from the willingness; that is to say, the International Law lies in the will of the State. There are different voluntaristic theories: the self-delimitation theory - which believes the State cannot oblige itself but has to be prior consent; the Vereinbarung - which says that the International Law is the result of the fusion of the willingness of the States in a common will; and the positivist theory - which believes in the intervention of the State from a formal point of view.
- Non-voluntaristic theory: It is founded on the idea that the International Law is not the result of a will. There also are different non-voluntaristic theories: The Natural Law - which believes that nature imposes some rules to human relations beyond any sort of social authority; the normative theory – which believes in a fundamental form (pacta sunt servanda) from which all other rules of law derive; and the sociologic school – which suggests the Law is derived from a social phenomenon that exercises a coaction imposed by the society to the individuals.
- Self-imposition theory: it believes that the State has sovereignty and cannot be subject to others' will, which does not mean the State cannot control its own will before others.
- Dogmatic theory: it believes that each legal system has a foundation that is complied with obligatorily. Its main objective to serve as the basis for the positivist Law, which entails the fundamental norm.

CLASSIFICATION OF THE SOURCES

The sources reveal the origins of the Public International Law. Its ruling essence does not result from a legislative body; its source is derived from the agreement of the subjects of International Law which is written in the treaties. As a discipline and a science, the Public International Law results from the theory of the knowledge which allows analysts to explain Law-related events in the grounds of international relations. Arthur Heffter, in his study of European Public International Law, suggested the sources of the International

Law were conventional laws that were either contained in the public treaties or «acknowledged by the European nations and their governments in their certain and constant use» (1875: 27).

From a normative point of view, the statute of the International Court of Justice, in the spirit of the law written in article 38, stipulates that the sources of International Law are:

1. The international treaties and agreements
2. The international custom
3. The general principles of the International Law
4. The legal decisions
5. The doctrine
6. The equality

International treaties or agreements

In compliance with the Vienna Convention on the Law of the treaties in 1969, a treaty is defined as «a written international agreement amongst States and ruled by the International Law, be it in an only piece or in two or more pieces linked regardless their denomination». Miaja de la Muela defines a treaty as «a declaration of bilateral or multilateral will issued by subjects of International Law» (1974:125).

With a different conception, Brotons believes that the treaty «is the source of international rights and duties» (1997:44). Charles Rousseau conceives two definitions of a treaty, one on an ample and other on a strict sense. On an ample sense, it may be defined as «every agreement made amongst members of the International Community» (p.23). On a strict sense, it is a «procedure to make an agreement; that is to say, its form, not the content» (1957:24).

Antonio Linares said a treaty is «an instrument in which freely agreed dispositions are made between two or more subjects of International Law in order to create, modify or expire rights and duties» (1992:62). We believe this definition is weak because the four variables therein described may be understood as the ones that define a contract. We adopt the definition contained in the Vienna Convention in 1969 and 1986 and we are aware it is a universal one. Nonetheless, as an added value, we would like to define a treaty as a convention predominantly legal amongst subjects of International Law in which the subjects in question manifest their interests to create rights and duties in order to meet the national States' high political, economic, social and cultural objectives.

The International Custom

Monroy Cabra defines the international custom as the «primary form of manifestation of the community, as it is formed by a set of rules of fact»

(1998:73). These rules are expressed in the reiteration of a series of compulsory acts contained in the *opinio iuris necessitatis;* that is to say, in the legal conviction that such behavior is obligatory. However, Defining the international custom as a source of the Public International Law leads us to revise the doctrine and legislation on the matter. In fact, the elements of the custom may be found in the doctrine: the material element or practice (*usus* or *diuturnitas*) and the spiritual element (*la opinio iuris*). That is why the international custom is composed by a permanent behavior that is linked to its obligatory condition.

As written by Max Sorensen (1985), the Public International Law was customary until not very long ago. The increase of international conventions, agreements and treaties is evidence of the importance of the custom as a source of International Law. However, the Kantian Statement declares the relations between the legal-natural links derived from a positive convention and the ontological variables that result from the manifestation of the international custom that has prevailed in the international relations. Article 38, extract b of the International Court of Justice stipulates that the international custom is evidence of the international practice generally accepted as law.

Truyol says the custom «is the primary form of manifestation of the positive will of a community: it is presented as a set of factually observed rules» (1977:25). These rules may be verified by the constant repetition of certain acts, together with the perception of being mandatory. Rodriguez Carrion confirms it when he says that the «customary rule is the result of a practice generally accepted as Law by the States (1998:241). We adjust to the healthy and accepted doctrine and define the international custom as the general acceptance of bureaucratic behavior - because it is derived from the national States - that becomes a legal-formal source of Public International Law, with the legal conviction that such behavior is necessary for the international community.

General Principles of the Law

The historiography of the Public International Law contains what happened in centuries XIX and XX when the general principles of the law were applied in the arbitration agreements spontaneously. This happened when an international arbitrator was unable to justify a decision in a treaty or custom and implemented a rule formulated in compliance with primary internal rights associated to their background and legal knowledge.

The general principles of the Law are material source of the Public International Law. Truyol defines it as the «ethical demands immediately and orderly applicable to the international relations of each period or historical situation. Such demands are valid regardless they may or may not be registered by the formal sources of creation of the International Law (1995: 105). Article 38 of the Statute of the International Court of Justice acknowledges such principles as a source of the International Law. However, we believe the aforementioned rule uses the phrase «civilized nations», when it refers to all kinds of civilization, including the western ones.

There are different positions in the study of the general principles of the Law as a source, starting with those who assure that there is international consciousness to those who say such principles result from the social custom of the nations. Today we believe the general principles of the Law are their auxiliary sources as well as the jurisprudence to be revised as follows.

Legal sentences

Throughout history, the value of the jurisprudence has been an alternative to analyze the Law, even before the codes and doctrine. The jurisprudence is not a direct source of the International Law because its decisions do not produce Law but rule it. Article 38 of the Statute of the International Court of Justice acknowledges the «partially auxiliary» condition of the jurisprudence in order to determine the rules of the Law.

The decisions issued by the International Court of Justice are auxiliary sources because they only compel the parties in litigation involved with the case in question. The doctrine stipulates that the court may adopt two categories of acts: the court order, which is related to the process of law; and the sentences or consulting decisions, which conclude the action of the court. Additionally, the decisions may be considered obligatory unilateral acts that stipulate rights and create obligations to third parties. These acts are compulsory for the parties, are definite and may also be revised by the court.

The doctrine

The doctrine is represented by the set of studies, opinions, administrative decisions, compilations and validly accepted treaties. Article 38 acknowledges the doctrine as an «auxiliary means» for the analysis and determination of the rules of Law. As we can see, it is not a formal source but an instrument and auxiliary resource of the Public International Law.

We have to differentiate the doctrines that produce legal knowledge in international matters as the result of the scientific-legal rationality. According to Article 38 of the Statute of the International Court of Justice, the doctrine is the opinion of the outstanding doctrinarians of the International Law. It entails the opinion of recognized institutions that have made important contributions to the formation and study of the International Law and its process of development and codification. Yet, after a careful revision of the normative classification of the sources in which we have to include the unilateral acts of Law, the treaty is to be studied in depth as a main source of the Public International Law.

The equality

The equality, defined as the direct application of the natural reason, is mandatory for the application of the rules of Law. The Statute of the International Court of Justice stipulates the obligation the Court has to act in compliance with the equality.

THE TREATIES

Conclusion

The conclusion of a treaty is the process of negotiation from which the parties agree on a matter of common interest. There are different forms of concluding a treaty:

- Bilateral: The Ministry of Foreign Affairs of a State and the diplomatic agent of another sign an agreement of common interest. This type of conclusion may also be done through special missions previously accredited (Linares, 1992).
- Multilateral restricted: In this case, some States compel each other in reciprocal agreement, for example, an economic integration treaty. This type of treaty is agreed amongst a limited number of States.
- Multilateral general: It may be negotiated in an international conference, a plenipotentiary conference called by an international organization, such as the treaty agreed in the conference of the United Nations about diplomatic relations and immunity.
- Simplified agreement: it is celebrated by exchange of notes and joint declaration, reciting general principles about one or several issues. It is a special manner to arrive at international agreements. It is not subject to ratification procedures and it is concluded by the ministers of foreign affairs, diplomatic mission heads and other State authorities (Ibid).
- Executive agreements: They involve two States and are not subject to ratification. They are based on a presidential prerogative (Ibid).

Effective date

The effective date indicates the moment in which the legal effects of the content of the treaty can be demandable by any of the parties. A treaty comes into effect on the date and form in which it is stipulated by the treaty or as agreed by the negotiating parties. When the effective date is not agreed for whatever reason, the consent of the negotiating States will be the only necessary requirement. The consent may be given after the effective date. In such case, the treaty will be valid for State as per the date of the consent - the effects may not be backdated (Monroy Cabra 1998).

The text of the Vienna Convention on the Treaties of 1969, which will be studied in the next chapter, rule the effective date of a treaty in article 24. It stipulates that a treaty will come into force in the manner and date agreed by the negotiating States. Additionally, it rules all aspects related to the consent. We will return to this topic as soon as we analyze the importance of such convention.

Classification of the treaties

The doctrine contains a rich and diverse classification of treaties. We are going to revise such diversity in a respectful manner towards what has been accepted academically and then we will present our own classification. Monroy Cabrera (1998:89) has suggested a classification as follows:

- Open and closed treaties: Open treaties allow the incorporation of other States while closed treaties are only joined by the signing States. The author uses the phrase «contracting party», which we are inclined to discard because it is not a contract but a treaty and both are ruled by different institutions of Law[10]
- Bilateral and Multilateral Treaties: Bilateral treaties are negotiated by two international subjects, while multilateral treaties are negotiated by two or more subjects. Monroy Cabra (Ibid) also suggests a classification based on the grounds of the treaty: political, academic, cultural, humanitarian or consular.

Charles Rousseau (1957) believes there are only two types of treaties that are interesting from a methodological point of view. He does a material classification in which there are two types of treaties: a *contract-treaty* that aims to establish a legal deal; and a *normative treaty* that aims to establish a rule of Law. He also does a formal classification in which there are bilateral and pluri-lateral treaties. This classification is founded on the number of States or subjects of Law participating in the negotiation.

Alvarez Londono (1998:69) suggests a similar classification to the previously cited. However, he innovates in the classification by derogation: *dispositive* and *imperative* treaties. Dispositive treaties stipulate possible conventional derogations, while imperative treaties nullify every treaty that conflicts with it.

Gaviria Lievano (1998) presents other classifications of treaties, beside the ones that are very similar to the previous ones, which is why we will not refer to all of them. We will refer to the law-Constitution and frame-Constitution. The first one stipulates the rules that may be applied to the organization it

[10] It is worth noting that a «contract treaty» is not a contract in strict sense, but a treaty.

creates exhaustively and it explicitly describes the attributions its components have that enable them to apply such rules. The second one does not only create an international organization but also enlists principles and provides general orientation about the policies that can be implemented in the field that it rules. Guerra Iguinez (1985), Sorensen (1985) and other authors have produced similar classifications to the ones we have previously referred to.

Whereas treaties may be classified as in two large groups - based on their subjects to the rule: bilateral and multilateral; based on the ruled object: humanistic (including the academic ones), humanitarian, scientific, social-economic and public health-related. We will now present the formalities that treaties should comply with based on the doctrine definitions we have previously referred to.

Conditions of form and content

The conditions of form and content of the treaties are part of what we call necessary conditioning elements for their existence. On this sense, there are two types of elements: the form elements - these are related to the validity of the treaties; and the content elements - these are related to those who can sign them and from which subjective rights are derived. The specificity of the formal elements are related to the stages of creation of a treaty, which may be presented as in the following chart:

<table>
<tr><th>Form Element</th><th>Stages</th><th>Principle</th></tr>
<tr><td rowspan="3">Initial phase</td><td>Negotiation</td><td>Negotiating pactum</td></tr>
<tr><td>Adoption</td><td>consensus</td></tr>
<tr><td>Authentication</td><td>willing to commitment</td></tr>
<tr><td rowspan="2">Final phase</td><td>manifestation of consent</td><td>formal confirmation</td></tr>
<tr><td>perfection of consent</td><td>ratification and incorporation</td></tr>
</table>

We will revise each of the stages for a better understanding of the process in an orderly manner.

Initial phase

Negotiation

Brotons elaborates on his speech about the content of the initial phase of creation of treaties by defining the negotiation as: «the participation in the creation of the text of a treaty by proposing, discussing, counter-offering or accepting suggestions for the clauses that will compose it» (1997: 205). Manuel Diez de Velasco defines negotiation in the context of the first phase of conclusion of treaties as the task «performed by the representatives of the parties for which offers, counter-offers and discussions are made» (1973:89). Additionally, he warns negotiations are the essence of the diplomatic method in itself. Vergara Molano defines negotiation as «a series of discussions and preliminary studies in which the will of the representatives of the States interested is manifested as well as other different interests are claimed to reach to a consensus» (1995: 123).

The doctrine contains different manners of negotiation[11]. Firstly, if the negotiation is bilateral, it should be done, for example, by the minister of foreign affairs and the diplomatic representative of a State. If the negotiation is multilateral, it is done in the realms of a conference or congress, such as the summit of the G-15 that was held in Caracas in February 2004. We define negotiation as the process of political, economic, cultural or social matter in which parties agree on satisfying their interests.

Adoption

It is the legal act that takes place immediately after the end of negotiations and in which negotiators manifest their agreement with the content. This is why adopting is the expression of the approval of the final writing of the text of the treaty. The Vienna Convention on the Law of the Treaties stipulates that a text is considered as adopted when all the negotiators accept the final writing of the treaty. As observed, the adoption is the normative and methodological expression of the consent.

Authentication

The linear sequence of the formal phase leads us to the authentication of what has been negotiated and accepted. The authentication may be defined as the formal and solemn legal act in which the negotiators certify the accuracy of the text of the treaty as well as its veracity and it is stipulated in a definite manner. The adoption and authentication of the treaty are both closely linked. There are two manners of authentication: the signature or acronyms of the signers and the *ad referendum* signature which is subject to confirmation (Brotons, 1997:207).

Final Phase

Manifestation of consent

Article 11 of the Vienna Convention stipulates that the consent to a treaty may be shown with a signature[12], the exchange of instruments that compose a treaty, the ratification (in the case of the States) or the formal confirmation (in

---

11 We specifically refer to the piece cited by Charles Rousseau (1957).
12 We will specifically refer to this later.

the case of the international organizations), the acceptance, the approval or incorporation, or any other manner previously agreed[13]. However, there has been plenty of reflection in the concepts about the consent in the doctrine, and it may be defined as the explicit will to sign an agreement from which subjective rights are derived for the parties.

Perfection of consent

It is the formal and solemn certification of the consent of the subjects to abide to at an international level. Article 16 of the Vienna Convention explicitly stipulates a manner of perfection of consent which is the notification of the willingness to consent to other parties or depositors.

Principles that rule the Law of the Treaties

The principles verse on the support and foundation of the life of an institution. The doctrine has traditionally stipulated the following ruling principles of the Law of the Treaties: *pacta sunt servanda, bona fide, ex consensus advenit vinculum* and *res inter alias acta.*

Pacta sunt servanda

It is considered the most important principle of the International Law. It stipulates that the treaties have to be complied with. On the same matter, Article 26 on the Law of the treaties in the Vienna Convention stipulates that «every treaty in force is obligatory for the parties and it has to be complied with in good faith».

Bona fide

This is the principle of good faith which is stipulated in article 26 of the Vienna Convention. The good faith is intended to encourage the respect to the prohibition to abuse of the Law. The abuse may be confirmed when a right is not used in good faith; that is to say, in contradiction with the legal system in force (Vergara Molano, 1995).

Ex consensus advenit vinculum

It contemplated the obligation as derivation of the consent as an absolute power. It is only by consent the States may be able to commit to international obligations. The State has to manifest its will through the bodies that have been enabled to participate in treaties (Ibid). This principle is currently being underestimated because there are obligations that have to be met with or without consent such as the nuclear inspections.

---

13 Reflection made by Brotons (1997).

Res inter alias acta

This principle stipulates that the treaties can only create an obligation for the negotiating parties. However, this principle is relative because there may be resulted rights and duties that do not only affect the involved parties but also third parties that have not been part of the creation of the treaty (ibid).

Effects of the treaties

As stipulated by the doctrine, the treaties have different effects. These may be classified as follows: effects on the parties by the application of the principle *pacta sunt servanda;* and the effects on third parties by the application of the principle *res inter alios acta.*

Effects on the parties

The Vienna Convention about the Laws of the Treaties, in compliance with the principle of *pacta sunt servanda,* stipulates that treaties are to be complied with in good faith because their compliance is stipulated for the parties. The effects for them are described as follows: in regard to the executive branch, the legislative branch, the judicial branch and individuals. The explanation of these effects is as follows:

Effects in regard to the executive branch

They stipulate a link between the Domestic Law and the International Law. This is due to the fact that a treaty is not an integrated part of the legal system of a State unless the rules of Domestic Law to provide it with validity and legal force and effect to make it legitimate (Mansilla, 1990:173). The State is to provide whatever is necessary to create sufficient internal legal foundation as to ensure it is legitimate. There is an exception related to human rights in the light of the principle of «progression». Article 19 in the Constitution of Venezuela stipulates the protection the State should provide towards the respect of human rights, for which the application and compliance with the treaties on this matter are obligatory.

Effects in regard to the legislative and judicial branches

A treaty may require it to be passed in the legislative body of a State. This means the force and effect the subjective rights derived from the treaties may need a new law to provide them more power within the legal system of a State. There would be two roles to play in the judicial branch: interpretation and application of the treaty (ibid).

Effects in regard to the individuals

The principle that governs the treaty may be incorporated to the Domestic Law. This enables the individuals as holders of rights and duties in a treaty. For example, an individual may sue a State in the Inter American Commission of Human Rights, which makes the individual a holder of rights. Additionally, the Statute of the International Court of Justice stipulates that the responsibility is individual, which means the individual is subject to duties as well. Other examples of this may be the courts for the former Yugoslavia, Rwanda and Sierra Leone.

Effects in regard to third parties

The application of the principle *res inter alios acta* means the treaties only produce a relative effect in regard to third parties because they are not affected or benefited by the treaty unless they specifically give their consent. The doctrine stipulates different manners to give consent. Brotons (1997:207) presents the following ones: ratification, signature, the exchange of the instruments that integrate the treaty, incorporation and approval.

Ratification

It is a solemn act that derives from the highest authority of the State and it is manifested in a documents in which the commitment to fully comply with the treaty is explicitly proclaimed. In the case of Venezuela, article 154 in the 1999 Constitution stipulates that:

> The treaties agreed or joined by the Republic may have to be approved by the National Assembly before they are ratified by the President of the Republic, except from those that aim to execute or excel pre-existing duties of the Republic, apply principles that have been acknowledged by it, execute ordinary acts in international relations or exercise powers the law has explicitly allocated on the executive branch

The constitutional rule explicitly sustains the President of the Republic is responsible for ratifying the treaties agreed by Venezuela. Such ratification entails its publication in the Official Gazette in compliance with the Venezuelan Domestic Law. Other authors such as Vergara Molano (1995) say the ratification is an act in which the treaty is accepted.

Signature

Firstly, it is a formal act; secondly, it is the confirmation of the willingness to abide to the treaty. The signature ad referendum involves the revision of the text by the government so that a decision on whether the duties are accepted is made. The signature as evidence of consent may be verified in two manners: when the treaty stipulates the force and effect of the signature and when the negotiating States do it as well.

The exchange of instruments that integrate the treaty

This manifestation of consent entails the existence of two or more instruments that are part of the treaty. The exchange represents the verification of consent by the interested parties (Brotons, 1997). The bilateral treaties often use the exchange of ratification letters. The multilateral treaties involve a deposit of an instrument of ratification by each State. An international organization is appointed as the depositary. The consent is not complete unless a notification of the instrument of ratification is provided (Vergara Molano, 1995).

The incorporation

This manner of consent enables other subjects that were not initially part of the treaty to join them on a later date. This means the incorporation entails the acceptance of third parties to an already negotiated treaty because they become part of it once it has come into force.

Acceptance and approval

The first one is a manifestation of consent that entails the coming into force of the treaty. The second one is the acceptance in itself and entails the consent of the States to comply with and be subject to the Law agreed in the treaty.

Interpretation of the treaties

We define the interpretation of the treaties as the cognitive process for which the treaty is analyzed, understood and explained either partially or fully to all parties involved. In compliance with the Vienna Convention, a treaty is to be interpreted in good faith, with the rationality required for the terms of the treaty and with a clear perspective of its objectives and purposes. With this in mind, the principle pacta sunt servanda is helpful for a better interpretation of the treaties. The aforementioned Convention stipulates the manner treaties should be interpreted:

- In good faith
- In its simple terms
- As a whole, including preamble and annexes.
- Complementary means of interpretation may be used such as reports prior to the treaty as well as the context in which it was agreed.
- If in doubt about its content, the sense that better fits the objectives and purpose of the treaty will be considered.

Disclaimers and grounds for nullity

The disclaimers may be defined as a legal international act in which a State notifies its intention of not being compelled by some of the clauses of a treaty or wishes to modify those that may be interpreted in some manner when ratifying, signing, accepting or approving such treaty. The doctrine stipulates that a disclaimer may be formulated at the ratification signing or incorporation to the treaty (Vergara Molano 1995).

The grounds for nullity in treaties may be defined as the result that affects the validity, legality and legitimacy of the treaty when conditions that threaten its viability are confirmed. The Viena Convention indicates what the causes for nullity of the treaties may be. They have been grouped in four categories:

1. The competence to manifest the will of the subject (Articles 46 and 47)
2. The validity of the consent (Article 51)
3. The action of an international crime (Article 52)
4. The illegality of the object (Article 53) (Brotons 1997)

Each category has been elaborated on as follows:

The competence to manifest the will of the subject

Brotons says that «The first cause for nullity as indicated in the Convention is the violation of stipulations in the Domestic Law related to the competence to represent the State in the participation of the treaty (1997:275). Yet, three conditions may have to be verified before the international consent of the State is considered null:

1. It affects «fundamentally important» rules of the State's Domestic Law
2. The rule in question is related with the competence to represent the State in treaties, not with the procedures
3. The violation of the rule of the State's Domestic Law is clear and evident to everyone.

Another condition enlisted in the Convention is the disregard of a specific restriction of a plenipotentiary. Article 47 stipulates that:

> If the powers of a representative to manifest the consent of State in a treaty have been subject to a specific restriction, the disregard of such restriction may not claimed as grounds for nullity of the consent manifested by such representative unless it is previously notified to the other negotiating States.

The rule clearly indicates that any restrictions to the powers of the representative should be notified to the negotiating States and prior to the consent.

The validity of the consent

This is one of the reasons for nullity stipulated in the Vienna Convention. It may be confirmed when a State has been coerced or mistaken to manifest its will in a treaty. Article 51 in the Convention refers to «coercion» as a variable for nullity. Other variables for nullity are «fraud» in Article 49 and «corruption» in Article 50.

The action of an international crime

Article 52 of the Vienna Convention stipulates that «A treaty is void if its conclusion has been procured by the threat or use of force in violation of the principles of international law embodied in the Charter of the United Nations.» The prohibition of conflict resolution by war is the confirmation that a treaty may not be produced by invasion, annexation or other acts that violate the peace.

The illegality of the object

A treaty containing a rule that conflicts with peremptory norms of the International Law may be void as stipulated in Article 53 of the Vienna Convention (Brotons, 1997).

Termination

Article 54 of the Vienna Convention stipulates two conditions for which a treaty and its effects may be terminated. First: if in conformity with the provisions of the treaty. Second: any time by consent of all the parties after consultation with the other contracting States. Article 55 stipulates the reduction of parties in a multilateral treaty to a number fewer than required for it to come into force. This is why a multilateral treaty may not be terminated if the number of parties involved is fewer than required unless explicitly indicated in the treaty.

Article 56 stipulates the means that should be made available for termination in compliance with the law, in case this is not specifically stipulated by the treaty. The assumptions considered by the conventions are: the willingness of the parties to admit the possibility of quitting and the inference of the right of quitting in the nature of the treaty. In such cases, the party should notify its wish to leave at least two months in advance.

Article 57 stipulates the assumptions for which verification a treaty may be suspended, in compliance with its content or the consent of the parties. Such assumptions are the same ones that may have to be verified for the termination of the treaty, which are stipulated in the previously cited Article 54. Articles 59 and 60 stipulate two different assumptions to study the possibility of termination of a treaty. The first one is a posterior treaty and the second one is the violation of the treaty in question.

OTHER SOURCES OF PUBLIC INTERNATIONAL LAW

Unilateral Acts of the States

Article 38 in the Statute of the International Court of Justice does not mention the unilateral acts of the states. However, these have been accepted as a source of the Public International Law when they entail international significance or are aimed to affect the international legal relationships (Sorensen, 1985). They may also be acts of Domestic Law that have an impact in the international community.

Diez de Velasco (1973) says a unilateral act is an expression of willingness of one sole subject of International Law, which validity does not depend on other legal acts and tends to produce effects on the subject that issues it as well as on third parties in given circumstances. The expression of willingness by one sole international subject is a conditioning variable to identify the existence of a unilateral act of Law. The acknowledgement of the States, which will be studied in depth further in this book, is a unilateral act of Law.

The resolutions of international organizations

These are legal acts from which subjective rights and obligations are derived. The doctrine stipulates different types of legal acts. Firstly, the acts that only entail the duty of in good faith verify the possibility of complying with the content of the rules of the organization. These acts are seen as a recommendation; yet, they are expected to be complied with. Secondly, the acts that do not entail an obligation per se, but determine a formal behavior on the States. Thirdly, the acts of obligatory compliance but leave the manner of execution to the member States. Fourthly, acts of obligatory form and content.

The sources derived from the scientific and technological progress

The development of communications and the effects of globalization are conditioning variables for the production of new sources of Public International Law. The sole consideration of the impact the Internet has produced in the relations amongst the humans and communities is evidence of the technological influence in the creation of the Law and its understanding in the new and ample field of the international politics.

Nowadays, the doctrine has been very careful at firmly identifying a typology of «new» sources of International Law. Nevertheless, we believe Internet, or the effects of certain events derived from its use, is evidence of its impact on the Law and the society. On the other hand, satellite communications enable to verify legal acts amongst representatives of subjects of Law, without having to travel long distances. Yet, the essence is the same.

CHAPTER III

CONSULAR AND DIPLOMATIC LAW

Diplomacy. Diplomatic Law. Consular Law
«The Generalized error produces law»

Paulus

DIPLOMACY

Concept

Almost all of the books on Diplomatic Law, including Philipe Cahier's masterpiece (1965), define Diplomacy as an academic discipline as well as an action in which there is a common place for the management of international relations through the negotiation. We believe negotiation is the place half-way between the persuasion used to have influence on a third party to achieve specific objectives and the imposition implemented with the force which is used to subdue an individual or a State, within the boundaries of the rules set unilaterally. The negotiation takes place in the grounds of the politics, in which the parties involved commit to making mutual concessions and to give up a part of their claims in order to achieve a common goal.

Origins

Harold Nicholson (1954) tells the origins of the diplomacy warning us that before the I World War (1914-1918), people in general only seemed to have an occasional interest in international relations. There were periods in which the foreign policy became a point of disagreement. However, a great deal of the population was not very interested in the principles of such policy, nor its methods or the means for which it was implemented. The premise was the foreign policy had to be founded on ineludible national necessities, for which it went beyond the struggle of the political parties. Foreign affairs were perceived as part of a specialized and esoteric study. This is why the direction of the foreign politics was delegated to the cabinet and its specialists. They were trusted to manage the national rights and interests through the methods and means they may find feasible and appropriate.

DIPLOMATIC LAW

In our effort to find a definition, it is necessary to revisit the term «diplomacy»[14] in the field of the Diplomatic Law, providing it with our own etymological interpretation. We believe the diplomacy is an action the States or governments take in order to conciliate their social, economic, political and cultural interests by negotiating in the context of the foreign politics in order to comply with the objectives of a national project underlying in the political system that builds the structure of power. Javier Perez de Cuellar suggests an interesting explanation of the origin of the word diplomacy:

> There are three etymological explanations for the word diplomacy: The Greek term diploma meaning to fold was used for the documents in tablets issued by the sovereigns to present to their emissaries; the same term was used for the duplicate or copy of the document of accreditation the emissary gave the recipient and which original remained in the prince's possession. The word was also used to refer to the two pages together that contained accreditation and instructions (1997:13)

The term provides the orientation for finding the concept of Diplomatic Law, which is the object of our study. This is why after having revised the multiple definitions available we believe Diplomatic Law is a branch of Public International Law which rules the diplomatic activity and constitutes the legal foundation for the diplomatic agent in order to comply with the ends and guidelines of the foreign policy as defined by the government institutions. Hence, we believe Diplomatic Law takes part of a special Law defined by the exercise of the diplomatic activity and with a specific role in the set of norms ruled by the international structure and its members.

On the other hand, authors such as Jose Sebastian De Erice and O'shea describe Diplomatic Law differently when they assure that «Diplomatic Law constitutes a legal, positive, voluntary and public system evidenced in its written manifestations» (Nicolson, 1954: 46). Ismael Moreno Pino cites Cahier to define Diplomatic Law as the «set of legal norms aimed to rule the relations amongst the different organizations of the subjects of International Law responsible for the foreign relations of such subjects temporarily or permanently» (2001: 21). Daniel Antokoletz defines Diplomatic Law as the «branch of Public Law that studies the relations amongst States regarding the administration of international affairs and their representation abroad» (1948: 58).

It is important to note that the main object of study of Diplomatic Law is to rule the activity produced by the organizations of international relations,

---

[14] For references on the historical evolution of the diplomacy, we recommend reading Contemporary Diplomatic Law (1962), by Philipe Cahier, in the Spanish version by Jose Vicente Torrente, Marcelino Ojeda and Julio Gonzalez Campos (1965).

the States and other subjects of Public International Law, amongst which the human being should be considered.

Diplomatic Law and Foreign Policy

Very few authors have in an integrated speech explained the relation between the foreign policy as a political action and as a public policy, the diplomacy as a mean or action, Diplomatic Law as the legitimating and certifying body of the legality of the action of the State and the diplomatic as the executor of the intents and purposes of the foreign policy. This relation is also ruled by Public International Law. This is how the foreign policy may be manifested through the political action, which is governed by the ideology of a regime or by the interests of given groups of power; or even through the public policy rationally formulated by a specialized elite which is capable of providing the mass or the groups that constitute a society with a coherent, digestible explanation of the ends, means, actions and results of the policies in question. The coherence and consistency of the foreign policy throughout the governments will determine if such policy was defined as a political or a public action, seeing they should somehow remain for a certain period of time.

The design of the foreign policy, oriented by the President of the Republic as stipulated by Constitutional mandate, is performed by the bureaucratic organizations explicitly created for the execution of the foreign policy. One of them is the Ministry of Foreign Affairs, which executes the policy via the Venezuelan diplomatic missions accredited in foreign governments. The field in which the «ideas» that are part of the policy are confirmed is the diplomacy, which is also manifested in a negotiation sub-system in place and performed by the diplomatic agent in order to defend the permanent and vital interests of the nation as well as the objectives in each topic and agenda in which the country gets involved. This process has a legitimating and certifying foundation that lies in Public International Law as well as in Diplomatic Law. The process can be illustrated in the following scheme:

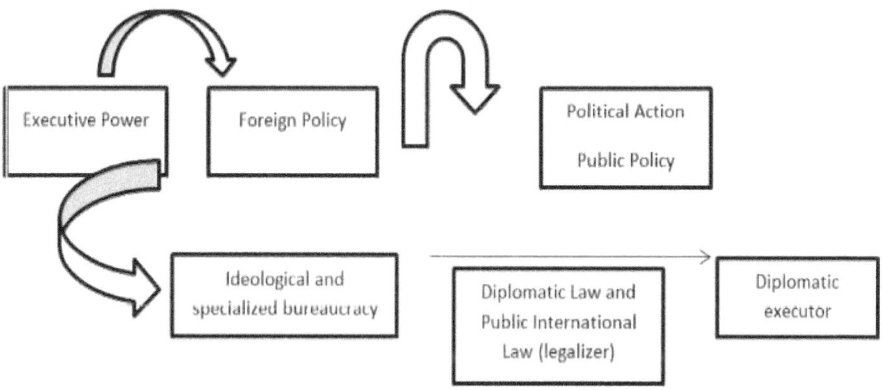

Diplomatic representations

The diplomatic representations are composed by the diplomatic missions and the members that are part of it. Its legal foundation lies in the subjective Law known as Mission Law. As stated by Perez de Cuellar (1997: 32), Mission Law is derived from a formal agreement amongst States in which, even though there is mutual acknowledgement, they are not obliged to accredit a mission or receive it unless they have formally committed to doing it. This Law takes place when the States agree on accepting permanent and special missions.

On the same matter, Morales Lesana defines each mission described in the doctrine and states that «the stable missions accredited in an international organization» or in a State are permanent (2000: 62), and their main aim is to represent the nation in the international organizations and keep the State informed of the activities of them in order to receive instructions from the government and get involved in the activities in question accordingly. On the other hand, The special missions are «sent to a State or International Organization in order to attend a specific affair or achieve a given objective» (p. 63).

However, the roles of a diplomatic mission may be defined as follows:

1. To represent the interests of the State by executing the actions of the foreign policy.
2. To strengthen the bounds of friendship and solidarity to consolidate the economic, cultural, scientific relations between its government and the receiving State, in compliance with the instructions received which would be based on the foundations of its foreign policy.
3. To produce reports about the political, economic, financial and commercial events happening in the receiving State and submit them to the Ministry of Foreign Affairs in a prompt manner.
4. To establish the processes for negotiation required with the receiving State about topics and agendas of common interest to meet the objectives of the foreign policy.
5. To comply with the norms of Public International Law that relate to the self-determination and no-intervention, as well as to defend the reputation and honorability of the nation it represents.
6. To promote the commercial, economic, cultural and social relations required to strengthen the bilateral initiatives between the nation it represents and the receiving State.
7. To promote the equality amongst the States, the peaceful solution of international conflicts, the cooperation, the respect to human rights, the solidarity amongst the peoples, the democratic practice in the

participation and decision-making within international institutions and organizations and to promote the Caribbean and Latin American integration, in compliance with the constitutional foundations for international relations and foreign policy in Venezuela.

Letter of Accreditation and Placet

The diplomatic representations are directed by a head of mission whose «appointment is communicated via letter of accreditation» (Moreno Pino, 2001: 145). The head of mission will present the communication to the receiving country's Head of State. The letter of accreditation is signed by the sending Head of State and then sent to the receiving country's Head of State and Minister of Foreign Affairs.

However, it is necessary to consult the appointment of a diplomatic representation confidentially through a process known as *Placet*, because no country is obliged to receive a chef of mission that may be considered susceptible to be objected. Once the consent is confirmed via the *agrément*, the appointment in question may be made public (Ibid). On the other hand, we may say there are two types of heads of mission: the political ones, which are identified with the regime in power; and the ones with a diplomatic background, which are familiar with the technical and bureaucratic elements of the job and have been incorporated into the diplomatic career via public entrance examination.

Privileges and diplomatic immunity

The privileges and diplomatic immunity are subjective rights of the diplomatic agents and are issued by the principle of reciprocity founded in the Vienna Convention on Diplomatic Relations. Such privileges and immunity protect the diplomatic agents against actions that may be addressed to them because of their roles of representation and protection. A diplomatic agent has the right to inviolability and immunity for criminal jurisdiction and special protection by the receiving State. This is also valid when an agent is in transit towards the country where their diplomatic tasks will be completed.

The jurisdiction immunity means the suspension of the effect of the law in the receiving State. The inviolability guarantees that no one take possession of the residence, office or files of the diplomatic agent, nor have access to them. Such privileges are also applicable to family members and official personnel of the mission. It is important to note that a diplomatic agent may never be exempt from the jurisdiction of the State they represent; that is to say, if a crime were committed, a diplomatic agent may be judged in their home country.

Every diplomatic agent is acknowledged the freedom of transit, communication and inviolability of their mail. In conclusion, the privileges and immunity diplomatic agents are entitled to, are ruled by the Vienna Convention on Diplomatic Relations, which will be studied in the following point.

Vienna Convention on Diplomatic Relations

The Vienna Convention on Diplomatic Relations came into force in 1961 but it was ratified and published in the Official Gazette N 27,612 in Venezuela on December 7th, 1964. The stipulations of the convention are ruled by the following principles:

1. The acknowledgement of ancient peoples of all nations of the diplomatic agents' statute.
2. The agreement on the purposes and principles of the Charter of the United Nations on the sovereign equality of the States, the peace keeping and international security, as well as the promotion of friendly relations amongst the nations.
3. The international convention on relations, privileges and diplomatic immunity will contribute with the development of friendly relations amongst nations, omitting the constitutional and social differences
4. The acknowledgement of the privileges and immunity with the aim of guaranteeing an efficient performance of the diplomatic missions to represent the States and not with the intention of benefiting individuals in particular.
5. The ratification of the norms of customary International Law will continue ruling the aspects that have not been explicitly ruled in the stipulations of the convention.

The first article of the Vienna Convention on Diplomatic Relations defines the terms that will be used in it:

- The members of the mission are the head of mission and the members of the personnel of the mission
- The head mission will be the person responsible for the sending State to act as such
- The members of the personnel of the mission are the members of the technical, diplomatic, administrative, and service members of the mission staff.
- The members of the diplomatic personnel are the members of the staff that possess a diplomatic status.
- The members of the technical and administrative personnel are the staff hired for administration and technical services of the mission.
- The diplomatic agent is the head of mission or member of the diplomatic staff of the mission.

- The members of the service personnel are staff members hired by the mission for household duties.
- A private housekeeper is a person responsible for the household duties of a member of mission - not an employee hired by the sending State.
- The facilities of the mission are the buildings or parts of a building, whoever the owner, used for the mission's purposes. This includes the residence of the head of mission as well as the land used for such building.

Diplomatic mission and the head of mission

Article 2 stipulates that the establishment of diplomatic relations amongst States and the creation of permanent diplomatic missions will be a free will act. On the other hand, articles 4 to 20 deal with the rules for the role of head of mission. Article 4 stipulates the conditions for the acceptance or rejection, stating that the sending State needs to make sure the person appointed for accreditation has been consented by the receiving State. The aforementioned article also stipulates that the receiving State is not compelled to explain the sending State the reasons for refusing to provide consent for a given proposed head of mission.

Article 5 stipulates three assumptions:

1. The sending State may accredit a head of mission for two or more States after having notified this to the receiving States. It can also send any member of the diplomatic staff to them unless a receiving State explicitly rejects it.
2. If a State accredits a head of mission for two or more receiving States, a diplomatic mission managed by an *ad interim* chargés d'affaires in each State in which the head of mission does not reside permanently.
3. The head of mission or any other member of the diplomatic staff of the mission will be able to represent the sending State in any international organization.

Article 6 stipulates the authority that two or more States have to accredit the same person as the head of mission in a third State; additionally, it also states the exception of «unless a third State refuses to it». The Convention does not stipulate the procedures for refusal; however, this should be done immediately, in the same act.

Article 7 stipulates the authority the sending State has to appoint the head of mission as well as the military, navy or air attachés. Article 8 identifies the conditions the members of the diplomatic should have:

1. They should have the nationality of the sending State.

2. They may not be chosen amongst people who have the nationality of the Receiving State, unless such State provides the consent, which may be withdrawn any time.

3. The receiving State may reserve the same right for the nationals from a third State which at the same time are not nationals from the sending State.

Persona *non grata*

In compliance with article 9, the receiving State may, at any time and with no explanation due, inform the sending State that the head of mission or another member of the diplomatic staff has been declared persona *non grata*, or that any other member of the mission is not acceptable. The sending State will withdraw the person in question or cease the person's roles and duties in the mission.

Any given person may be considered *non grata* or not acceptable prior to their arrived to the territory of the receiving State. If the sending State refuses to execute or does not execute within reasonable time their inherent obligations, the receiving State may deny the acknowledgement of the person as a member of the mission.

Number of members in the mission

Seeing there isn't an explicit agreement about the number of members in the mission, the receiving State may demand that the number be within the limits of what is considered reasonable and normal, depending on the circumstances and condition of the State and the needs of the mission in question. The receiving State may also refuse to accept agents of certain category, within those limits and without discrimination of any sort. The sending State may not open offices that are part of the mission in places different from where the mission is located without the explicit consent of the receiving State.

Notification to the Ministry of Foreign Affairs

The following aspects will be notified to the Ministry of Foreign Affairs regarding the receiving State:

1. The appointment of the members of the mission, arrival and departure as well as the cease of their roles in the mission.

2. The arrival and departure of every family member of a mission's member, or the fact that a person has become part, or has ceased to be part of a family of a mission's member.

3. The arrival and departure of the private housekeeper serving the people referred to in number 1 and, if applicable, the termination of their service.

4. The hiring or dismissal of people that reside in the receiving State as members of the mission or private housekeepers that have access to rights such as privileges or immunity.

Effect of the letters of accreditation

The stipulation contained in article 13 states two assumptions that explain the effect of the letters of accreditation:

1. The head of the mission is considered as having taken up his functions in the receiving State either when he has presented his credentials or when he has notified his arrival and a true copy of his credentials has been presented to the Ministry for Foreign Affairs of the receiving State, or such other ministry as may be agreed, in accordance with the practice prevailing in the receiving State which shall be applied in a uniform manner.
2. The order of presentation of credentials or of a true copy thereof will be determined by the date and time of the arrival of the head of the mission. This allows identifying the precedence of the agent within the diplomatic body accredited in the receiving State.

Precedence and classes of heads of mission:

Article 14 stipulates the three classes of heads of mission: ambassadors or nuncios accredited to Heads of State, and other heads of mission of equivalent rank; envoys, ministers and internuncios accredited to Heads of State; and chargés d'affaires accredited to Ministers for Foreign Affairs.

The precedence of the heads of mission will be determined in each class by the date and time of the arrival of the head of the mission, in compliance with article 13. The modifications of the letters of accreditation for a head of mission that do not entail a change of class will not alter the precedence. The stipulations of this article may be understood notwithstanding the uses the receiving State accepts regarding the precedence of the representative of the Holy See. The head of mission will notify the Ministry of Foreign Affairs, or any agreed Ministry, the order of precedence of the members of the diplomatic mission.

Absence of the head of mission

If the post of head of the mission is vacant or if the head of the mission is unable to perform his functions a chargé d'affaires ad interim shall act provisionally as head of the mission. The name of the chargé d'affaires ad interim shall be notified, either by the head of the mission or, in case he is unable to do so, by the Ministry for Foreign Affairs of the sending State to the Ministry for Foreign Affairs of the receiving State or such other ministry as may be agreed.

In cases where no member of the diplomatic staff of the mission is present in the receiving State, a member of the administrative and technical staff may, with the consent of the receiving State, be designated by the sending State to be in charge of the current administrative affairs of the mission.

The premises of the missions

The premises of the mission shall be inviolable. The agents of the receiving State may not enter them, except with the consent of the head of the mission. The receiving State is under a special duty to take all appropriate steps to protect the premises of the mission against any intrusion or damage and to prevent any disturbance of the peace of the mission or impairment of its dignity. The premises of the mission, their furnishings and other property thereon and the means of transport of the mission shall be immune from search, requisition, attachment or execution.

Tax exemption

The sending State and the head of the mission shall be exempt from all national, regional or municipal dues and taxes in respect of the premises of the mission, whether owned or leased, other than such as represent payment for specific services rendered. The exemption from taxation referred to in the Vienna Convention shall not apply to such dues and taxes payable under the law of the receiving State by persons contracting with the sending State or the head of the mission.

Additionally, diplomatic agents will be exempt from all dues and taxes, personal or real, national, regional or municipal, except:

1. Indirect taxes of a kind which are normally incorporated in the price of goods or services.
2. Dues and taxes on private immovable property situated in the territory of the receiving State, unless he holds it on behalf of the sending State for the purposes of the mission.
3. Estate, succession or inheritance duties levied by the receiving State, subject to the provisions of paragraph 4 of article 39; which is about a member of mission's pass away.
4. Dues and taxes on private income having its source in the receiving State and capital taxes on investments made in commercial undertakings in the receiving State.
5. Charges levied for specific services rendered.
6. Registration, court or record fees, mortgage dues and stamp duty, with respect to immovable property, subject to the provisions of article 23, which is about the taxes derived from services delivered.

Communication with the missions

Article 27 of the Vienna Convention stipulates seven variables that rule the communication with the missions:

1. The receiving State shall permit and protect free communication on the part of the mission for all official purposes. In communicating with the Government and the other missions and consulates of the sending State, wherever situated, the mission may employ all appropriate means, including diplomatic couriers and messages in code or cipher. However, the mission may install and use a wireless transmitter only with the consent of the receiving State.

1.1 The official correspondence of the mission shall be inviolable. Official correspondence means all correspondence relating to the mission and its functions.

1.2 The diplomatic bag shall not be opened or detained.

1.3 The packages constituting the diplomatic bag must bear visible external marks of their character and may contain only diplomatic documents or articles intended for official use.

1.4 The diplomatic courier, who shall be provided with an official document indicating his status and the number of packages constituting the diplomatic bag, shall be protected by the receiving State in the performance of his functions. He shall enjoy person inviolability and shall not be liable to any form of arrest or detention.

1.5 The sending State or the mission may designate diplomatic couriers ad hoc. In such cases the provisions of paragraph 5 of this article shall also apply, except that the immunities therein mentioned shall cease to apply when such a courier has delivered to the consignee the diplomatic bag in his charge.

1.6 A diplomatic bag may be entrusted to the captain of a commercial aircraft scheduled to land at an authorized port of entry. He shall be provided with an official document indicating the number of packages constituting the bag but he shall not be considered to be a diplomatic courier. The mission may send one of its members to take possession of the diplomatic bag directly and freely from the captain of the aircraft.

Privileges and immunity of the diplomatic agent

The person of a diplomatic agent shall be inviolable. He shall not be liable to any form of arrest or detention. The receiving State shall treat him with due respect and shall take all appropriate steps to prevent any attack on his person, freedom or dignity. The private residence of a diplomatic agent shall enjoy the same inviolability and protection as the premises of the mission. His papers, correspondence and, his property, shall likewise enjoy inviolability. A diplomatic agent will also be entitled to the following immunity:

1. A diplomatic agent shall enjoy immunity from the criminal jurisdiction of the receiving State. He shall also enjoy immunity from its civil and administrative jurisdiction, except in the case of: (a) A real action relating to private immovable property situated in the territory of the receiving State, unless he holds it on behalf of the sending State for the purposes of the mission; (b) An action relating to succession in which the diplomatic agent is involved as executor, administrator, heir or legatee as a private person and not on behalf of the sending State; (c) An action relating to any professional or commercial activity exercised by the diplomatic agent in the receiving State outside his official functions.

2. A diplomatic agent is not obliged to give evidence as a witness.

3. No measures of execution may be taken in respect of a diplomatic agent except in the cases coming under subparagraphs (a), (b) and (c) of paragraph 1 of this article, and provided that the measures concerned can be taken without infringing the inviolability of his person or of his residence.

   3.1. The immunity of a diplomatic agent from the jurisdiction of the receiving State does not exempt him from the jurisdiction of the sending State.

   3.2. The immunity from jurisdiction of diplomatic agents and of persons enjoying immunity may be waived by the sending State. Such waiver must always be express.

4. The initiation of proceedings by a diplomatic agent or by a person enjoying immunity from jurisdiction shall preclude him from invoking immunity from jurisdiction in respect of any counterclaim directly connected with the principal claim.

   4.1 Waiver of immunity from jurisdiction in respect of civil or administrative proceedings shall not be held to imply waiver of immunity in respect of the execution of the judgment, for which a separate waiver shall be necessary.

Other associated privileges and immunity

The members of the family of a diplomatic agent forming part of his household shall, if they are not nationals of the receiving State, enjoy the privileges and immunities specified as follows: they shall not be liable to any form of arrest or detention, their residence and personal effects shall enjoy inviolability, shall enjoy immunity from the criminal jurisdiction of the receiving State, shall also enjoy immunity from its civil and administrative jurisdiction and shall enjoy tax exemption.

Members of the administrative and technical staff of the mission, together with members of their families forming part of their respective households, shall, if they are not nationals of or permanently resident in the receiving State, enjoy the privileges and immunities specified in articles 29 to 35, except that the immunity from civil and administrative jurisdiction of the receiving State specified in paragraph 1 of article 31 shall not extend to acts performed outside the course of their duties. They shall also enjoy the privileges specified in article 36, paragraph 1, in respect of articles imported at the time of first installation.

Members of the service staff of the mission who are not nationals of or permanently resident in the receiving State shall enjoy immunity in respect of acts performed in the course of their duties, exemption from dues and taxes on the emoluments they receive by reason of their employment and the exemption contained in article 33.

Private servants of members of the mission shall, if they are not nationals of or permanently resident in the receiving State, be exempt from dues and taxes on the emoluments they receive by reason of their employment. In other respects, they may enjoy privileges and immunities only to the extent admitted by the receiving State. However, the receiving State must exercise its jurisdiction over those persons in such a manner as not to interfere unduly with the performance of the functions of the mission.

Duration of the privileges and immunity

Every person entitled to privileges and immunities shall enjoy them from the moment he enters the territory of the receiving State on proceeding to take up his post or, if already in its territory, from the moment when his appointment is notified to the Ministry for Foreign Affairs or such other ministry as may be agreed.

When the functions of a person enjoying privileges and immunities have come to an end, such privileges and immunities shall normally cease at the moment when he leaves the country, or on expiry of a reasonable period in which to do so, but shall subsist until that time, even in case of armed conflict. However, with respect to acts performed by such a person in the exercise of his functions as a member of the mission, immunity shall continue to subsist.

In case of the death of a member of the mission, the members of his family shall continue to enjoy the privileges and immunities to which they are entitled until the expiry of a reasonable period in which to leave the country. In the event of the death of a member of the mission not a national of or permanently resident in the receiving State or a member of his family forming part of his household, the receiving State shall permit the withdrawal of the movable property of the deceased, with the exception of any property acquired in the country the export of which was prohibited at the time of his death. Estate, succession and inheritance duties shall not be levied on movable property the presence of which in the receiving State was due solely to the presence there of the deceased as a member of the mission or as a member of the family of a member of the mission.

Innocent passage

If a diplomatic agent passes through or is in the territory of a third State, which has granted him a passport visa if such visa was necessary, while proceeding to take up or to return to his post, or when returning to his own country, the third State shall accord him inviolability and such other immunities as may be required to ensure his transit or return. The same shall apply in the case of any members of his family enjoying privileges or immunities who are accompanying the diplomatic agent, or travelling separately to join him or to return to their country.

Third States shall not hinder the passage of members of the administrative and technical or service staff of a mission, and of members of their families, through their territories. Third States shall accord to official correspondence and other official communications in transit, including messages in code or cipher, the same freedom and protection as is accorded by the receiving State. They shall accord to diplomatic couriers, who have been granted a passport visa if such visa was necessary and diplomatic bags in transit, the same inviolability and protection as the receiving State is bound to accord.

The obligations of third States under paragraphs 1, 2 and 3 of this article shall also apply to the persons mentioned respectively in those paragraphs, and to official communications and diplomatic bags, whose presence in the territory of the third State is due to force majeure.

End of functions of a diplomatic agent and end of a diplomatic mission

The function of a diplomatic agent comes to an end when there is a notification by the sending State to the receiving State that the function of the diplomatic agent has come to an end; or on notification by the receiving State to the sending State that, in accordance with paragraph 2 of article 9, it refuses to recognize the diplomatic agent as a member of the mission.

If diplomatic relations are broken off between two States, or if a mission is permanently or temporarily recalled, the receiving State must, even in case of armed conflict, respect and protect the premises of the mission, together with its property and archives. The sending State may entrust the custody of the premises of the mission, together with its property and archives, to a third

State acceptable to the receiving State. The sending State may entrust the protection of its interests and those of its nationals to a third State acceptable to the receiving State.

Optional Protocol concerning the Compulsory Settlement of Disputes

It was approved by the United Nations Conference held in Vienna, from March 2nd to April 14th 1961. This protocol stipulates the obligation to attend the Criminal Court of Justice in case of a conflict derived from interpretations or applications of the Convention, unless the parties have agreed on an arrangement within a reasonable period of time.

CONSULAR LAW

Concept

A contemporary definition that may more closely describe the Consular Law may link it with the branches of the Domestic Law, which main role is to rule the activities of the society in their public and private relations. This is why its proximity to Constitutional, Administrative, Tax and Civil Laws not only place it as a branch of International Law but also as an external appendix of Domestic Law regarding people, goods and private and public economic relations.

The Ecuadorian author Carlos Puig Vilazar defines Consular Law not only as an appendix of «Public International Law but also as the extension of Political and Administrative Law, because its content includes principles of internal State regime and its practice entails the Domestic Laws of the States, because they stipulate the rules of the consular service» (1970: 9). On the other hand, in compliance with the generally accepted doctrine, the sources of the Consular Law are the treaties or conventions in place amongst the States that have a consular relation, the laws of the State that receives the consular agent, the laws of the sending country, the laws of the receiving country, the principle of reciprocity, the use and the custom.

Historical reference

If we consider the secondary sources that contain information about the history of the Consular institution, its origin may be traced back to the period of the crusade, which collides with the development of the trade in the Mediterranean Sea. However, its background is actually much older - it goes back to ancient time.

According to Herotodus[15] (1968), the Greeks established a judge in Naucratis that resolved the conflicts in compliance with their own laws. The Greeks created two institutions: the Prostates and the Proxeny. The first one

[15] Greek Historian (Halicarnassus, 484 – 426 B.C.).

provided the foreigners in Greece with the right to choose a protector amongst the Greeks (Prostates) in order to act as intermediary in their relations with the State. The Proxeny was for a foreign country what the Prostates was for an individual. It was based on a contract agreed between the State and a citizen from another State, for which the citizen became an official protector of the government that appointed them as well as the interests of their nationals.

Years later, in the imperial Rome, the institutions became more flexible after the predominance of the concepts of Roman citizen, Quiritary right and foreigners as enemies prevailed for years. Schemes with a more human nature appeared: The Hospitium, the Patronage and the Pretor Perenigrus. The majestic Greek civilization was in its last days and the Proxenie had virtually disappeared. We can trace back the appearance of the *consul in partibus ultra marini*, a name used to call the agent that was sent from a State or city to another State or city to protect the trade and resolve the conflicts amongst their nationals. We can also find the first code that ruled over the rights and duties of the consuls with the name of Amalfi tables, from centuries XI to XIV.

The consuls

We have found the pieces produced by the Dominican ambassador Manuel Morales Lesama[16], particularly useful throughout the bibliographic revision made to present the ideas herein contained. According to him, the consular service is «the one that is performed in order to promote the trade between the country and the territory of jurisdiction (and) to protect the people and their national interests as it happens» (p. 82). We believe the consul is an agent of promotion of trade which protects, represents and promotes the general security of the nationals from the State they represent, regarding the defense of the interests of their State.

Organic Law of the Consular Service

The Organic Law of the Consular Service was issued on 21 August 1987 and contains 67 articles that rule the consular activity and the agents that perform it. Article 1 stipulates the authority of the Executive Power to accredit consular agents to other nations in compliance with treaties and international conventions sourced by the international practice or the principle of reciprocity. This is a clear sign of the subordination of Consular Law to Public International Law, seeing it contains the legal foundation of the international action within its dichotomist nature: diplomatic and consular.

Article 2 stipulates the place of residence of the general consul, which is the capital city or any other important city within the jurisdiction. Additionally,

---

16 His masterpiece Diplomacia Contemporanea, teoria y practica (2000) allows us taking his opinion I full, as they are part of a Latin-American approximation to the study of the Diplomatic and Consular Law.

the content of the law indicates the authority of the Executive Power to accredit more than one general consul to a nation in case there is a considerable distance between them or under special circumstances.

Articles 3 to 5 stipulate the hierarchy of the General Consul and their roles as the «head of consular agents within their district», which main duty is to supervise the compliance of their subordinates' duties, who are independent in the performance of their roles but have the obligation to keep an open communication with the General Consul and produce reports for them about the activities in their consular offices. As the head of the consular agents, the General Consul has the duty of promptly informing the Ministry of Foreign Affairs and the corresponding mission any irregularities observed in the consular and vice-consular agents under their supervision.

Articles 6 to 10 stipulate the requirements, obligations and characteristics of the consular agents, which may be summarized as follows:

1. Consular agents should be Venezuelan at birth
2. They will report all aspects related to the income produced by the consular offices to the Ministry of Finance. If no tax duties are due, they will report to the Venezuelan mission accredited in the country in which they have been assigned.
3. Their signature of authorization is not delegable or transferable.
4. Their post is to be performed in their office and any act performed out of the consular office will be rendered as null.
5. They will be under oath and will do what is required to ensure a positive performance of their duties.

Attributions of the consular agents

The attributions of the consular agents are contained in article 11 in the Consular Service Law. They are described in 38 numbers which explain the behavior and duties of the consular agents in general, and allowing a freer interpretation of other alternative duties performed to satisfy the needs of Venezuelan citizens in transit or residing in the countries where the consular agents have been allocated. The aforementioned points stipulate that the duties of the consular agents are:

1. To watch over the interests of the country and protect the rights and interests of the Venezuelans.
2. To protect the trade of the Republic and promote its expansion, as well as to fight the smuggling with Venezuela.
3. To lead very well addressed publicity campaigns, presentations and similar events through the media to promote exportable Venezuelan

products by taking different initiatives that enable such products to gain credit and position in the local market.

4. To visibly keep graphic information available in the consular office about the cities, ports, public monuments, museums, leisure places, hotels and other elements that contribute with the increase of the tourism in Venezuela - profitable source for the nation - and provide all sorts of information about it.

5. To keep a database of the Venezuelans that reside in their jurisdiction, to register those who wish to be included in it as well as the children to Venezuelans born in their jurisdiction, in which case a legal copy of the birth certificate is to be sent to the Ministry of Foreign Affairs.

6. To keep a roll call of the Venezuelans residing in their jurisdiction and send a copy of any changes in it to the mission and the Ministry of Foreign Affairs every month.

7. To certify the behavior of the Venezuelans living in their jurisdiction.

8. To certify the status of public health at the departure of ships sailing to Venezuela and confirm the health authorization issued by the port authorities, in compliance with the maritime health in force.

9. To issue passports and visas to Venezuelans and foreigners in compliance with the international scheme followed by the Venezuelan government and to certify all requirements, especially the period of validity.

10. To ask for instructions to the Ministry of Foreign Affairs or the corresponding mission about underprivileged Venezuelans who may be unable to return to the country, meticulously specifying what the background of the person is.

11. To authorize the transit and legal shipping of merchant vessels going to Venezuela.

12. To ensure no abuse or fraud is committed on the nation's flag's behalf.

13. To allow the loading and unloading of crew sailors in Venezuelan ships for justified reasons.

14. To certify the origin, provenance and quality of any shipped goods.

15. To prohibit the delivery of goods and products considered a public health risk or harmful and report it to the Venezuelan government.

16. To scrupulously comply with the stipulations of the law and rules of the Health Maritime Venezuelan Police.

17. To intervene as an arbiter in the conflicts amongst their nationals or between their nationals and foreigners.

18. To resolve any inconveniences between captains and crew in Venezuelan merchant ships.
19. To prosecute crimes committed in off shore or on national ships by rectifying or expanding the procedure and submit them, together with the guilty ones, to the relevant authorities.
20. To efficiently cooperate with the seizure of deserters from national war ships.
21. To determinedly protect Venezuelan merchant ships in compliance with the law.
22. To inform the government about the arrival of criminals prosecuted by the country.
23. To inform about people accused of crimes in other countries departing for the Republic; or any other person that may be rendered as harmful for the country, in compliance with the laws on admission and expulsion of foreigners.
24. To inform about the financial status of the banks, companies and other corporations or commercial institutions with business operations with Venezuela.
25. To inform about the financial status, respectability and business performance of companies or individuals residing in their jurisdiction with contracts agreed with the Venezuelan government.
26. To represent Venezuelans who are absent and there is no one who can represent them if the protection of their interests or their personality is required; as well as to watch for the rights of Venezuelans residing in their jurisdiction to the authorities of the country where they are accredited.
27. To promote the creation of charity organizations amongst the Venezuelans who reside in their jurisdiction.
28. To receive and record any claims, protests, counter-protests made by Venezuelans and captains of merchant ships to preserve own and else's interests and responsibilities and to report it to the Ministry of Finance.
29. To legalize the signatures of local authorities when required.
30. To inform the government in detail about any punishable act committed by a Venezuelan in their jurisdiction, as well as the outcome of the judgment.
31. To inform the Ministry of Finance about any events against the tax laws done by a ship.

32. To impede any hostile acts against the peace of the country with the support of the local authorities.
33. To inform the government about any events related to the public order.
34. To report the government about mandates of tax or any other nature, as well as events that may have a direct or indirect impact on the country's trade.
35. To inform the Ministry of Foreign Affairs about ships' flags changes.
36. To instruct the captains of Venezuelan ships to let disadvantaged Venezuelan sailors on board in order to take them back to the country.
37. To report the accounts, balance and income from consular rights to the Ministry of Finance and the Exam Office within the dates and through the instruments stipulated by the law. Such income is to be cashed in the public registry office and the documents records are to be sent by the consular office and their rights will be complied with when introduced in the country.
38. To comply with other stipulations contained in the law.

The Consular Service Law stipulates other consular agent duties such as: ordinary and special reports to the Ministry of Foreign Affairs about economic and commercial activities in the countries where they reside (articles 12 and 14); the obligation to fly the flag in national holidays (article 17); the obligation to keep political neutrality in the country where they reside (article 18); and duties related to succession (articles 23 to 39).

Consular immunity and prerogatives

Consular immunity and prerogatives are stipulated in the Vienna Convention on Consular Relations, which has been ratified by Venezuela. These privileges include the use of the national flag and shield, the inviolability of the premises, files and other consular documents, freedom of transit and communication and taxes and consular rights.

The Convention also stipulates what follows in article 41 about the inviolability of the person:

1. Consular officers shall not be liable to arrest or detention pending trial, except in the case of a grave crime and pursuant to a decision by the competent judicial authority.
   - 1.1 Consular officers shall not be committed to prison or be liable to any other form of restriction on their personal freedom save in execution of a judicial decision of final effect.
   - 1.2 Proceedings shall be conducted with the respect due to him by reason of his official position.

Additionally, the Convention stipulates consular agents hold immunity to the jurisdiction; therefore they are not subject to the authorities of the receiving State.

Letter Patent

Letter Patent is a document in which a sending State accredits a Consular Agent as such. It is to be issued for each appointment, and the class, category, location of the consular office and the full name of the consular agent will be therein indicated. The Letter Patent will be issued by the sending State for the receiving State. If accepted, the sending State will submit a notification to the receiving State with the identification of the new consular agent. The admission or authorization the receiving State provides for the consular agent is known as exequatur.

Venezuelan Foreign Service

Venezuelan Foreign Service[17] is a highly demanding professional role for those who start a career in this field after successful approval of a competitive examination entrance. The law stipulates the admission to Foreign Service through a competitive examination entrance in the sixth category. The Foreign Service Law from 2001 derogates the norms that had been in force since 1961. There are six categories in the Foreign Service:

1. First diplomatic category: Ambassador
2. Second diplomatic category: Minister-counselor
3. Third diplomatic category: Counselor
4. Fourth diplomatic category: First Secretary
5. Fifth diplomatic category: Second Secretary
6. Sixth diplomatic category: Third Secretary

We may summarize the most important changes regarding the diplomatic personnel as follows:

1. Professionals with a bachelor's degree or equivalent are allowed to opt for the examination entrance to be admitted in the Foreign Service starting in the Third Secretary category. No age limits are stipulated, as opposed to the previous law, which stated a minimum age of 30 years old.
2. As per the coming into force of the Law, a process of revision of credentials is performed in order to incorporate commissioned agents that gather the academic requirements and the length of service.

[17] Fermin Toro Jimenez makes an interesting historical revision regarding the evolution of the Venezuelan foreign service in his piece Derecho Internacional Publico (2001).

3. The Executive Power reserves the right to appoint 30% of the diplomatic agents who will be enabled to perform the assigned tasks for a maximum period of three years.

CHAPTER IV

LATIN-AMERICAN LEGAL FOUNDATION

Considerations about International Society and Law
Venezuelan legal nature

Law is a common provision.

Papianus

CONSIDERATIONS ABOUT INTERNATIONAL SOCIETY AND LAW

Regarding the concept

The conceptual revision analyzed by Brotons (1997:1) about both the international society and law, gives up the positivist criteria traditionally incorporated to the discussion about the existence of International Law. On this matter, we appointed a few considerations in Chapter I about the concept of Public International Law that suggest the existence of different elements, according to which the concept may contain multiple definitions.

Brotons questions himself the existence of International Law and simultaneously proposes a definition in which we identify two elements that condition a factual existence of this Law: «legal provisions ruling certain relations (rights and obligations)» and the existence of members in the international society to which he qualifies as subjects because of the acknowledgment of an international subjectivity.

Regarding the rejections

The central idea regarding the rejections looked over by Brotons denies the legal capacity of International Law *(Ibid)*, supporting the idea in the lacking of a coercive capacity in its internal background, therefore, the unenforceability of its external background. Regarding the criteria of Austin *(Ibid:2)* he proposes the comparison made by the latter, suggesting that its ruling capacity derives from the moral or international courtesy, incapable of imposing real sanctions but ethical ones.

On the other hand, he considers that if such legal capacity exists (quotation which he considers pathetic) it may imply to contemplate the usage of the strength as a similar element of a sanction. On this ground, he considers that such affirmation would equal to acknowledge the usage of the strength from the States with enough means to dominate the weakest ones in order to «legitimate the causes of the most powerful ones» *(Ibid)*. So, he gives up such rejection concluding that the in existence of International Law «it is essential the existence of an International Society» *(Ibid)*. On this matter, we consider the aforementioned not sufficient to reconsider the existence of a Public International Law as it must be added the coexistence of «what is conventional, free and explicit», from which can derive the mutual consensus to be subject to jurisdiction.

Regarding the International Society: conditioning elements

Brotons (1997:4) suggests that not only is the international society a conditioning element to the existence of an International Law, but also a factual circumstance of the consent of the interested subjects. This quotation confirms the initial weakness pointed by Brotons by defining International Law when he considers that the existence of the conventional makes possible for the States to fulfill by themselves 3 purposes: creation, jurisdictional verification and execution of Law. These considerations can be added also to the criteria which considers that «the lack of institutions in the International Society may strengthen the role splitting of its members [which considers that the States] when acting on his own [they do it also] on behalf of the International Society» *(Ibid)*.

We support this criteria based on the not-less-conservative point of view, according to which the most powerful States are capable of invoking the «role splitting» to act based on their own interest. In addition, we have to point out that this realistic point of view is an expression of an international structure in which the «society» element is composed by States that head their actions based on maintaining their national security (Morgenthau, 1963).

Regarding the enforceability of International Law

It is pretty common to (re)think about the enforceability of International Law, even to awareness the indiscriminate use of the force which constantly violates and diminishes what we assume conceptually exists and should be factual evidenced. It results in the need to invoke the epistemological theory of Public International Law as an object of study by reviewing 3 existing elements: provisions, consent (conventional element) and self-decision-making power.

It turns out idealistic to believe that, according to the principle of good faith *(bona fide)* the powerful States would give up on *(exconsensu advenit vinculum)* the use of the strength to submit themselves to what was agreed among the parties *(pacta sunt servanda)* or if a legal or real reason cause impact to third parties *(res inter alios acta)* (p. 71). In fact, a realistic approaching would impose the criteria that the States would never give up on pursuing their interests and to do so, they would invoke the use of force as an expression of real power in order to fulfill their real and potential needs.

Regarding the spontaneous compliance to infringement and aggravation of International Law: worldwide?

Continuing the quotation made by Brotons (1997:6) regarding the conflict between Iran-Iraq, that shows the struggle between consent (explicit, inexistent or impertinent) and the interests at that time, the aforesaid author states that the obligations, to which the States are subject to, must be sufficiently explained to prevent the opposition, denial or (counter) interpretation of the law from happening throughout the conventional act. This situation, besides getting us closer to a legal utopia, puts us in front of a complex, difficult and violent reality in which clarity, as a secondary element, must support the rules that creates the obligations from the Law is derived.

Actually, the universalization of Law is a historical process, as well as social, economic, political and cultural, which divides its territorial scope in legal, international and regional principles -as in American International Law- or in thematic-ideological principles (politic-ideological: power-interests). This leads us into a consideration of a real and necessary existence of imperative international provisions that can be accepted voluntarily by the States, of the monistic relation, in which National Law makes possible the existence of an International Imperative Law until the international society evolves (because of a historical fact) towards a Universal Law that allows the dualistic existence and evidences, simultaneously, the real and conceptual existence of a non-questionable and non-refutable International Law.

VENEZUELAN LEGAL NATURE

Principal provisions

It is a common opinion to consider every State's Constitution as the logical and enforceable foundation that gives life to Public International Law. In fact, the Venezuelan system on Public International Law is statutory, as well as Private International Law[18]. Nonetheless, this opinion is still on debate.

The national legal foundation from which Public International Law in Venezuela is supported is the Constitution of the Bolivarian Republic of Venezuela, published in the extraordinary Official Gazette number 5.453, on March 23rd 2000. The Constitution stipulates in article 152 the principles that must conduct the

[18] See El Sistema venezolano de Derecho Internacional Privado (1996) by Juan Maria Rouvier.

international act and, therefore, inspire the consent in the creation of the sources of Public International Law. Those principles are detailed as follows:

1. Independence.
2. Equality among States.
3. Self-determination and non-intervention.
4. Cooperation.
5. Respect Human Rights.
6. Solidarity among people.
7. Democratic practice in the participation and decision-making on the grounds of International Organizations.
8. Promotion of the Latin-American and Caribbean integration.

The legislator considers that the progress and creation of Public International Law provisions must be founded in these principles, expressed on the approved, executed and ratified treaties by the Republic. On this matter, we consider that the legal nature of Public International Law regulations is in a Constitutional level. Let's now analyze each one of these principles and the impact caused towards the foundation of Public International Law.

Independence

Independence, on the internal order, suggests the autarchic capacity of a State to execute its sovereignty in order to promote the political regime and governance system that be a society's unique expression and reflection of its political culture. On the external order, suggests that the authorities and governance system shall not be subject to the interests and dominance of any foreign country. It means that all States have the power to execute the international agreements considered necessary to fulfill their national interests, without any other interests than those ruled by their institutions and legal governments lawfully established being applicable.

On the other hand, we have to advise that independence does not grant a State the authority to repudiate the provisions ruling the International Community, so it must be subject to the principles of universal peace and respect to Human Rights governing all Nations. Despite the diversity of cultures ruling all Nations, we also consider these principles cannot be replaced by invoking the States' Independence, seeing the foundation of its axiological values corresponds to the liberal idea of equality, which is coherent with the human reason of providing a primary position of respect to all manifestations of human being's freedom.

Equality among States

It is the political result of the Independence of States. Some authors (such as Garcia Venturin, 1979:243) consider that equality as a synonym of justice.

However, when we analyze the concept, we notice the existence of two types of equality: the lawful and desirable one, which commands the responsibility to giving people what they deserve -this quotation is closer to the idea of Justice-; and the real equality one, which demands that it should be distributed to match individual merits and needs. If we explore this concept in the international field, it is observed that in front of diminishing unequally realities, this principle is just a guidance meant to promote social-economic cooperation towards the most powerful countries.

The duty the world has to assist the weakest ones from the wealthiest and most powerful Nations makes us ask ourselves a moral question: can we talk about equality among the States when there are societies facing what we know as starvation, while others have massive resources which make possible a surplus in their citizens' life style?

The answer makes us evaluate the defining elements in the wealth distribution among the Nations and the disproportionate power that the strongest ones have over the weakest ones, imposing cultural, political and economic practices. In any case, it would be unfair to affirm that the principle of equality is applied to all Nations. Nonetheless, our legislation stipulates such principle as a guideline to define the national interest since in the face of the Nations, Venezuela considers that its relations with other States must be set by a fair and equal treatment, regardless the social, political, economic and cultural performs of the rest of the Nations.

Equality among States has also another background from the Declaration regarding the principles of International Law, which refers to friendly relations and cooperation among states, stipulated in resolution 2.625-XXV of the General Assemble of the United Nations in 1970.

Self-determination and non-intervention

Self-determination and non-intervention entails respect to sovereignty. This principle is sustained by articles 10 and 11 of the Charter of the American States. Such articles stipulate that «every American State has the duty to respect the rights enjoyed by every other State in accordance with international law [and must be respected] the fundamental rights of States [which] may not be impaired in any manner whatsoever»

On the other hand, the Venezuelan Constitution assumes, as this principle is stipulated, that the Venezuelan Foreign Policy must be subject to the respect of self-determination and non-intervention. So, that keeps the custom imposed in Venezuela with the non-intervention doctrine, approved by Antonio Jose de Sucre in 1828 (Toro Jimenez, 2001:566).

The principle of non-intervention has certain boundaries regarding to what should not be interpreted in the sense that no act can affect the dispositions of the United Nations related to maintenance of peace and inter American security (Remiro Brotons, 1997:888). On this matter, we agree with the opinion of Brotons, as he states that «the principle of non-intervention, which has a secant relation with the one who forbids threatening and the use of strength, has a tangential relation with the influence that some States have on others as a normal and legal result of diplomatic practice» (1997:84).

Additionally, Guerra Iniguez (1985:108) explains the historical background of the principle of non-intervention:

> The non-existence of the right to intervention gives rise to the enforcement of the principle of non-intervention. This principle was born in the middle of XIX century as a result of the abuse committed by the great powers due to his interventionist practices, which they justified based on different reasons. In 1823, the Monroe Doctrine was released which, simultaneously, was supported by the anti-interventionist policy of Great Britain, which had been opposing to interventionist practices of the Holly Alliance since 1815. From that time on, the principle of non-intervention has been evolving flawlessly, due to the historical and sociological background of the American International Community, which is different to the European once. As a matter of fact, Europe is an International Community set by the experience of States duly organized in different manners from each other. It means that next a Monarchy a republic was governing as well, a Kingdom or an Empire, and in a State were coexisting a multitude of nationalities separated from each other for religion, culture and social prejudices matters (1985:399).

On this ground, we consider that the Monroe Doctrine, previously quoted by Guerra Iniguez *(Ibid)*, besides promoting the principle of non-intervention, was stated a policy of non-intervention oriented by the interests of the United States Foreign Policy. That is why we consider the pragmatism of non-intervention and respect to self-determination of the States is determined by the equilibrium of power over the world order, bearing in mind that those States with major military capacity always tend to disrespect the aforesaid principle. We have to bring up the multiple cases of intervention that we have seen over the last few years, in which the UN has not been efficient enough to impose some type of sanction to restore the state of freedom of a State, therefore the duty to reestablish the order has been left in the hands of nations with that power of real action.

Peaceful solutions to international conflicts

It is an answer to an ontological aspiration of the States: the pursuit of peace and establishment of means and methods to obtain it. However, this aspiration is an answer to an expressed mandate of the United Nations through which it is imposed that all legal controversies be subject by the parties to the

International Court of Justice. On the other hand, if it is related to de facto acts and means that disturb international peace, the Security Council shall facilitate the ideal ways to resolve the controversies.

Regarding this principle, it is important to bring up the dichotomist interpretation made by Rodriguez Carrion between Law and social reality. This author considers that as long as Law is born from stability and permanence advocacy, social reality is normally changing (1998:109). This states clearly the imminence of conflicts in the international society, which is even more dynamic as it entails «many social realities» interacting with each other. That is why the national legislation points out that to the possibility of international conflicts in which Venezuela may be involved; it is a constitutional mandate to resolve them through peaceful means and methods stated in the regulations of Public International Law.

Cooperation

In International Relations and Political Science cooperative games make possible that both players obtain reciprocal retributions. That is why the legislator imposes to the authorities in charge of the Foreign Policy the obligation to cooperate in regards of 2 coincident elements: to facilitate the Latin-American and the Caribbean processes (which is a constitutional mandate) and to obtain a reciprocal treatment in the cooperative relations from friendly Nations.

Respect to Human Rights

This principle corresponds to the American Convention on Human Rights or «Pact on San Jose Costa Rica» mandate, which the Venezuelan legislator has adopted as approbatory law, since Human Rights has preeminence and precedence over the Constitution. This means that the international treaties on this field are directly applied over constitutional elements, and also that they fulfill with the principle of «progressivity» on Human Rights. So, the Statement of Reasons in the Constitution in force (1999) states that:

> ...inspired by the principal tendencies that have been developed in Common Law and international treaties on Human Rights, it is recognized the principle of progressivity on the protection of such rights and the State shall grant every legal or natural person, without any form of discrimination its respect, enjoyment and inexorable right, indivisible and independent of such rights.

Furthermore, the legislator recognizes «the Constitution, international treaties validly subscribed by the Republic on this field and the rules stipulating so, as the sources on the protection of Human Rights».

Insisting on the importance of this topic, the legislator stipulates that regarding the strengthening the protection of such rights, it is stated that all international treaties, pacts and conventions subscribed and ratified by Venezuela, prevail in the internal order, as long as it contains more favorable provisions about enjoyment and exercise of human rights than the provisions contained in the Constitution and other regulations, so that the dispositions be direct and immediately applied by the Courts of the Republic and other bodies of the Public Power. Therefore, as long as a treaty contains dispositions that guarantee certain human right in a wider and more favorable manner than the Constitution, it shall prevail and be applied in a direct and more favorable manner by the Courts and other bodies of the Estate.

Solidarity among people

It is the ontological content of the pragmatic cooperation. While solidarity aims for equity and justice at the moment of the relation, cooperation aims for shared earnings. Solidarity among people goes from the cultural to the economic. It does not expect retribution from the receiving State, but contains the principle of reciprocity whenever necessary. Solidarity contains the idea of good neighbor over good will.

Democratic practice in the participation and decision-making on the grounds of International Organizations

Participatory and protagonist democracy is the legal and political sustain of the constitutional project, from which the foreign action of Venezuela shall adjust itself to the principles stated in Public International Law. By virtue of that fact, it has been developed a policy that defends the democratization of international organizations in the pursuit of multipolarity. This policy corresponds to the principle of the democratic practice on participation and decision-making on the grounds of International Organizations.

Promotion of the Latin-America and Caribbean integration

The State aspires to reach an economic, social and political in Latin America and the Caribbean, to face the challenges of this century. Its spirits looks back to the Bolivarian thoughts and Congress of Panama, over which a policy of approximation and approaching to make possible better relations among the peoples' neighbors is scaled. It is aspired to incorporate in the world all Latin American and the Caribbean nations capable of competing alongside the extra continental great powers. Those principles are developed within a strategy aimed for the defense of sovereignty and promotion of a multipolar international society. In this sense, the political regime has formulated the «social economic developing plan» which we reproduce herein regarding the international area:

> On criminal matters: the international criminal matter is not a new field. It treats all that is related to national and international crimes that violate human rights, aimed for the responsible ones be taken before the justice

and processed at the instance of the Security Council. On this matter, we are referring to the International Criminal Court. The creation of such jurisdictional instance was part of the agenda of the UN since 1948, but it was not until the massacres of Rwanda and the former Yugoslavia, when its consolidation process was sped up.

In regards to the crimes that may be upraised to international instances, the Venezuelan Criminal Code stipulates in its internal legislation the following felonies also listed in the international field:

1. Piracy (article 153).
2. Weapons' collecting, persons' recruitment and expeditions with hostile means (article 154).
3. Breaking of ceasefire in a war (article 156).
4. Violation of international treaties and agreements that put in risk the responsibility of the Republic (article 156).
5. To penetrate the geographic space of a friend Nation (article 157).
6. Felonies against the first Magistrate of a foreign Nation (article 158).
7. Felonies against the representatives of the First Magistrate (article 160)
8. Destruction of the flag and other representative of a foreign Nation (article 159).

On civil matters: section IV, title I of the Civil Procedural Code stipulates the international procedural jurisdiction. In addition, the purpose of the law states the importance that jurisdictional bodies get on letters rogatory matters. It is important to mention that such international jurisdictions are easily confused when it comes to cases that subrogate themselves in regulations of Public International Law, hence in our case the topics relating the national States to international procedural matters, gain great relevance.

Approbatory Law of the American Convention on Human Rights. Pact of San Jose, Costa Rica

This law was published on the Official Gazette number 31.256, on June 14th 1977. The purpose of this law stipulates all aspects related to Human Rights. The preamble states that the purpose of the Convention[19] is the defense and consolidation, within the framework of democratic institutions, a system

[19] Subscribed by Colombia, El Salvador, Jamaica, United States, Honduras, Dominican Republic, Argentina, Mexico, Uruguay, Guatemala, Peru, Costa Rica, Haiti, Trinidad and Tobago, Ecuador, Barbados, Paraguay, Panama, Brazil, Chile, Bolivia, Nicaragua and Venezuela.

of personal liberty and social justice based on respect for the essential rights of man. This law stipulates in its domestic law what have been agreed upon by the States in International Law, which is the reason they are obliged to. This is a clear representation of the dualism we analyzed in previous chapters. It is also important to remember the origin of Pact of San Jose which is set forth in the Charter of the Organization of American States (1967), in the American Declaration of the Rights of Man and in the Universal Declaration of Human Rights. Let's now analyze the bonding elements of this rule with Public International Law.

Firstly, the States recognize the existence of an international society integrated for divergences of race, color, sex, language, religion and ideology. Therefore, the rule imposes «the obligation to respect the rights» derived from the Convention and the domestic law approved in its Internal Legislation, without any distinction. In addition, all human beings are recognized as a person.

Secondly, in a dualist conception, the norm stipulates that in those States in which there is no legation that promotes equality, are obliged to implement all necessary legislative policies to sanction a law that guarantees the respect to such rights. We will study the approbatory law as an element that explains dualism in the Venezuelan system of Public International Law, when dealing with the topic of Human Rights further ahead.

Inter-American Democratic Charter

As quoted by Jaime Ordonez, professor at Universidad de Costa Rica, the Democratic Charter «is an instrument created to fill the legal flaws presented in the Charter of the OAS, and some other substantive resolutions of the democratic system of the States members on different hypothesis to a simple coup d'etat» (2001:23). His opinion summarizes the essence of the assumptions that founded the creation of the Charter in study. In fact, despite the current weakness of the OAS, the Democratic Charter is an expression of the power that the topic of democracy has as an instrument of political cohesion for the achievement of processes of integration, as it is expected to fill the legal flaws set forth in the Democratic Charter of the OAS and in resolutions such as the 1.080.

The Inter-American Democratic Charter was approved in the first plenary session of the twenty eighth extraordinary sessions of the General Assembly of the OAS at Lima, Peru, on September 11th. The 19 assumptions that set the foundations for the promulgation of such Charter were:

1. It recognized that representative democracy is indispensable for the stability, peace, and development of the region, and that one of the purposes of the OAS is to promote and consolidate representative democracy, with due respect for the principle of non-intervention.

2. The contributions of the OAS and other regional and sub-regional mechanisms to the promotion and consolidation of democracy in the Americas were recognized.

3. The Heads of State and Government of the Americas, gathered at the Third Summit of the Americas, held from April 20 to 22, 2001 in Quebec City, adopted a democracy clause which establishes that any unconstitutional alteration or interruption of the democratic order in a state of the Hemisphere constitutes an insurmountable obstacle to the participation of that state's government in the Summits of the Americas process.

4. Existing democratic provisions in regional and sub-regional mechanisms expressed the same objectives as the democracy clause adopted by the Heads of State and Government in Quebec City.

5. The participatory nature of democracy in our countries in different aspects of public life contributed to the consolidation of democratic values and to freedom and solidarity in the Hemisphere.

6. Solidarity among and cooperation between American states required the political organization of those states based on the effective exercise of representative democracy, and that economic growth and social development based on justice and equity, and democracy are interdependent and mutually reinforcing.

7. The fight against poverty, and especially the elimination of extreme poverty, was essential to the promotion and consolidation of democracy and constitutes a common and shared responsibility of the American states.

8. The American Declaration on the Rights and Duties of Man and the American Convention on Human Rights contain the values and principles of liberty, equality, and social justice that are intrinsic to democracy.

9. The promotion and protection of human rights is a basic prerequisite for the existence of a democratic society, and recognizing the importance of the continuous development and strengthening of the inter-American human rights system for the consolidation of democracy.

10. Education is an effective way to promote citizens' awareness concerning their own countries and thereby achieve meaningful participation in the decision-making process, and reaffirming the importance of human resource development for a sound democratic system.

11. A safe environment is essential to the integral development of the human being, which contributes to democracy and political stability.

12. The Protocol of San Salvador on Economic, Social, and Cultural Rights emphasizes the great importance of the reaffirmation, development, improvement, and protection of those rights in order to consolidate the system of representative democratic government.

13. The right of workers to associate themselves freely for the defense and promotion of their interests is fundamental to the fulfillment of democratic ideals.

14. In the Santiago Commitment to Democracy and the Renewal of the Inter-American System, the ministers of foreign affairs expressed their determination to adopt a series of effective, timely, and expeditious procedures to ensure the promotion and defense of representative democracy, with due respect for the principle of nonintervention; and that resolution AG/RES. 1080 (XXI-O/91) therefore established a mechanism for collective action in the case of a sudden or irregular interruption of the democratic political institutional process or of the legitimate exercise of power by the democratically-elected government in any of the Organization's member states, thereby fulfilling a long-standing aspiration of the Hemisphere to be able to respond rapidly and collectively in defense of democracy.

15. In the Declaration of Nassau [AG/DEC. 1 (XXII-O/92)], it was agreed to develop mechanisms to provide assistance, when requested by a member state, to promote, preserve, and strengthen representative democracy, in order to complement and give effect to the provisions of resolution AG/RES. 1080 (XXI-O/91).

16. In the Declaration of Managua for the Promotion of Democracy and Development [AG/DEC. 4 (XXIII-O/93)], the member states expressed their firm belief that democracy, peace, and development are inseparable and indivisible parts of a renewed and integral vision of solidarity in the Americas; and that the ability of the Organization to help preserve and strengthen democratic structures in the region will depend on the implementation of a strategy based on the interdependence and complementarity of those values.

17. In the Declaration of Managua for the Promotion of Democracy and Development, the member states expressed their conviction that the Organization's mission is not limited to the defense of democracy wherever its fundamental values and principles have collapsed, but also calls for ongoing and creative work to consolidate democracy as well as a continuing effort to prevent and anticipate the very causes of the problems that affect the democratic system of government.

18. The Ministers of Foreign Affairs of the Americas, at the thirty-first regular session of the General Assembly, held in San Jose, Costa Rica, in keeping with express instructions from the Heads of State and Government gathered at the Third Summit of the Americas, in Quebec City, accepted the base document of the Inter-American Democratic Charter and entrusted the Permanent Council of the Organization with strengthening and expanding the document, in accordance with the OAS Charter, for final adoption at a special session of the General Assembly in Lima, Peru.

19. All the rights and obligations of member states under the OAS Charter represent the foundation on which democratic principles in the Hemisphere are built, and the progressive development of international law and the advisability of clarifying the provisions set forth in the OAS Charter and related basic instruments on the preservation and defense of democratic institutions, according to established practice.

Democracy and the Inter-American system

The peoples of the Americas have a right to democracy and their governments have an obligation to promote and defend it (article 1).

The political history of our peoples has been characterized by autocracy[20], authoritarianism, militarism, coup d'etats and civil wars. It was not until the end of the XX century when many Latin-American countries understood the need to pursuit of stability. In Venezuela, the democratic profile aspired with the electoral victory of the writer Romulo Gallegos finally got -after the defeating of Marcos Perez Jimenez- an apparent stability on the hands of the elected President Romulo Betancourt and the named Betancourt Doctrine[21] That is why assuming democracy as a right, represents la victory of political liberalism in the West against militarist tendencies that in the seventies upraised in our continent, such as the case of Videla and his Board of 1976, in Argentina; the case of Pinochet, in Chile; and the case of Banzer, in Bolivia[22].

---

[20] Note from translator: we have found autocracy may be the word that best describes the concept used by the author in the original text. Caudillismo is a word used to refer to the tendency of believing in charismatic but autocratic leaders. It has been said this is a strong tendency in the history of Latin American politics.

[21] See La Politica exterior del gobierno de Rómulo Betancourt (1959-1964) by Luis Manuel Marcano Salazar (1998:84 and 85).

[22] Even though the inspiration from which Brazer had the desirte to re-take the power came from Venezuela's motivation, especially during de government of Carlos Andrés Pérez (1974-1979), which lead to the foundation of Acción Democrática Nacionalista party and afterwards let him reach the power in 1997.

Democracy and rule of law

Article 2 states the following:

> The effective exercise of representative democracy is the basis for the rule of law and of the constitutional regimes of the member states of the Organization of American States. Representative democracy is strengthened and deepened by permanent, ethical, and responsible participation of the citizenry within a legal framework conforming to the respective constitutional order.

The effective exercise of representative democracy is an ideal. It is as to speak for justice, equity and well common. Actually, representative democracy makes possible that majorities put in a few the necessary confidence to provide them with the sovereign power residing in the peoples.

The essential elements of representative democracy

> Essential elements of representative democracy include, inter alia, respect for human rights and fundamental freedoms, access to and the exercise of power in accordance with the rule of law, the holding of periodic, free, and fair elections based on secret balloting and universal suffrage as an expression of the sovereignty of the people, the pluralistic system of political parties and organizations, and the separation of powers and independence of the branches of government (article 3).

Democracy, heir of Liberal state, has been an achievement for the future of the Latin American peoples. Political differences and antagonist practices in regards to a scope of freedom and democracy have caused the institutional breakup and have ruined fundamental principles in most of our nations, such as those the Inter-American Democratic Charter safeguards. For that reason, the protection offered by this Charter to representative democracy is constituted in the hub for the achievement of Latin-American modernization and development.

Argentina, Paraguay, Uruguay, Chile, Ecuador, Bolivia, Peru, Colombia and Venezuela have witnessed, at different stages of history, de upcoming of authoritarian regimes, regularly militarist, that have violated public liberties and human rights. That is why the Charter states that consubstantial elements of representative democracy include human rights, fundamental liberties and the holding of periodic, free and fair elections based on secret balloting and universal suffrage as an expression of the sovereignty of the people.

The exercise of democracy

Article 4 states that:

> Transparency in government activities, probity, responsible public administration on the part of governments, respect for social rights, and

> freedom of expression and of the press are essential components of the exercise of democracy.
>
> The constitutional subordination of all state institutions to the legally constituted civilian authority and respect for the rule of law on the part of all institutions and sectors of society are equally essential to democracy

The weakening of democracy is originated, mainly, by the profanation of public confidence. People -who exercise it through suffrage-, must trust in their institutions and holders that, representing them, exercise public functions in the pursuit of well common, justice and legal security. It must be added the capacity and faculty that the peoples have to express themselves freely and the existence of a legitimate opposition to a government for the establishment of the equilibrium of internal power.

Political parties

Article 5 in the Inter-American Democratic Charter states:

> The strengthening of political parties and other political organizations is a priority for democracy. Special attention will be paid to the problems associated with the high cost of election campaigns and the establishment of a balanced and transparent system for their financing.

Duverger (1965) stipulated that political parties are the base and foundation of representative democracy. On this matter, the Charter imposes the obligation to strengthen such parties. Nonetheless, knowing the history of political parties in Latin America and the economic deterioration that many nations suffer as a consequence of the crisis that has affected the continent in the past years, it is suggested, for a well distribution of wealth, the establishment of an equilibrium that allows the election campaigns cuts and a transparent financing. It also involves the purpose of avoiding the temptation of many politicians to finance their campaigns with funds from drug trafficking or any other illegal source.

Citizen participation

Regarding citizen participation states that:

> It is the right and responsibility of all citizens to participate in decisions relating to their own development. This is also a necessary condition for the full and effective exercise of democracy. Promoting and fostering diverse forms of participation strengthens democracy.

Democracy resides in the people, who exercise it through universal suffrage. This constitutional principle is not dead letter. The survival of democracy as a system and manner of life depends on citizen participation, not only on the election of representatives of the government, but also as controllers of such purpose and producers of public opinion.

Democracy and Human Rights

> Democracy is indispensable for the effective exercise of fundamental freedoms and human rights in their universality, indivisibility and interdependence, embodied in the respective constitutions of states and in inter-American and international human rights instruments (article 7).

As we have stated, there cannot be a democratic regime if it is not sustained on the respect of Human Rights. It is considered indispensable the existence of institutions that respect y make respect such rights in all ways.

Claims for violation of Human Rights

> Any person or group of persons who consider that their human rights have been violated may present claims or petitions to the inter-American system for the promotion and protection of human rights in accordance with its established procedures.
>
> Member states reaffirm their intention to strengthen the inter-American system for the protection of human rights for the consolidation of democracy in the Hemisphere (article 8).

A great achievement we have to state was promoted by Romulo Betancourt: the recognition of representative democracy as a model of political life for the Latin-American nations. Consubstantiated with that ideal, Human Rights are included. Who of us have not read or been witnesses of violation of Human Rights? Throughout this article, any person who considers themselves violated in the respect of Human Rights may exercise an action by claim.

Elimination of all forms of discrimination

> The elimination of all forms of discrimination, especially gender, ethnic and race discrimination, as well as diverse forms of intolerance, the promotion and protection of human rights of indigenous peoples and migrants, and respect for ethnic, cultural and religious diversity in the Americas contribute to strengthening democracy and citizen participation (article 9)

It is utopic to think that man will eliminate of their intellectual and construct the prejudices. Even though cultural and social discriminations seem to be overcome, what we have to face today in Latin America is the political discrimination. On this ground, the Constitution is very clear by forbidding all forms of discrimination and actions against human nature.

Workers and democracy

Article 10 stipulates:

> The promotion and strengthening of democracy requires the full and effective exercise of workers' rights and the application of core labor standards, as

recognized in the International Labour Organization (ILO) Declaration on Fundamental Principles and Rights at Work, and its Follow-up, adopted in 1998, as well as other related fundamental ILO conventions. Democracy is strengthened by improving standards in the workplace and enhancing the quality of life for workers in the Hemisphere (article 10).

The International Labour Organization is an institution that produces Law. From an international point of view it obliges States to adopt actions intended to produce wellbeing to workers. Workers, as fundamental piece of a legal organized society, are at the same time fundamentals for the existence of representative democracy.

Democracy, Integral Development and Combating Poverty

Democracy and social and economic development are interdependent and are mutually reinforcing (article 11).

Democracy is a political system of life, consubstantial with social and economic development of the men. In a social state of Law where poverty prevails, despite the labor force the men put to develop themselves, it cannot be spoken about the existence of a real and effective democracy.

Poverty and Education

Poverty, illiteracy, and low levels of human development are factors that adversely affect the consolidation of democracy. The OAS member states are committed to adopting and implementing all those actions required to generate productive employment, reduce poverty, and eradicate extreme poverty, taking into account the different economic realities and conditions of the countries of the Hemisphere. This shared commitment regarding the problems associated with development and poverty also underscores the importance of maintaining macroeconomic equilibria and the obligation to strengthen social cohesion and democracy.

The promotion and observance of economic, social, and cultural rights are inherently linked to integral development, equitable economic growth, and to the consolidation of democracy in the states of the Hemisphere (articles 12 and 13).

The fight against corruption and poverty has been the promise made by Latin American politicians who have not been able to fulfill after they are in power. Bernardo Kliksberg (1993) has stated in many opportunities, and also written in his pieces, that the fight against poverty is a non-postponed topic, suggesting that it depends on the development of Latin American peoples. Wisely, members of the OAS have seen the need to implement consubstantial policies to human factor that allow bureaucracies develop actions to dignify the existence of citizens in economically equilibrated societies. It will make the birth of stable democratic regimes in the region possible.

Dialogue and combat against poverty

Member states agree to review periodically the actions adopted and carried out by the Organization to promote dialogue, cooperation for integral development, and the fight against poverty in the Hemisphere, and to take the appropriate measures to further these objectives (article 14).

Social equilibrium is product if the dialogue among the different sectors of society and cooperation among nations. On this matter, member States of the OAS are constituted in social controllers in regards to the promotion of dialogue and instruments of cooperation that allow an integral development of societies. It will contribute, evidently, with the policies implemented to combat poverty in the hemisphere.

Sustainable development and democracy

The exercise of democracy promotes the preservation and good stewardship of the environment. It is essential that the states of the Hemisphere implement policies and strategies to protect the environment, including application of various treaties and conventions, to achieve sustainable development for the benefit of future generations (article 15).

Every democratic political regime must watch for the protection of the environment as a natural space over which societies grow and develop. The OAS considers that sustainable development is indispensable for the establishment and consolidation of democratic regimes.

Education and democracy

Education is key to strengthening democratic institutions, promoting the development of human potential, and alleviating poverty and fostering greater understanding among our peoples. To achieve these ends, it is essential that a quality education be available to all, including girls and women, rural inhabitants, and minorities (article 16).

Education policies for democracy are indispensable for the strengthening of democratic institutions. Those policies depend on formal education reaching everyone, in terms of establishing a solid base for the construction of a society with solid foundations in familiar, social and political education.

Strengthening and Preservation of Democratic Institutions

Articles 17 and 18 refer to democratic institutionalism as stating that:

When the government of a member state considers that its democratic political institutional process or its legitimate exercise of power is at risk, it may request assistance from the Secretary General or the Permanent Council for the strengthening and preservation of its democratic system. When situations arise in a member state that may affect the development of its democratic political institutional process or the legitimate exercise of power, the Secretary General or the Permanent Council may, with prior consent of the government concerned, arrange for visits or other actions in order to analyze the situation. The Secretary General will submit a report to the Permanent Council, which will undertake a collective assessment of the situation and, where necessary, may adopt decisions for the preservation of the democratic system and its strengthening.

Risk of democratic institutionalism dissolution is arisen by member states with preventive measures. On this ground, States will the Secretary General or Permanent Council know about the possible loss of the constitutional and democratic order.

Procedure to preserve democratic institutionalism

Based on the principles of the Charter of the OAS and subject to its norms, and in accordance with the democracy clause contained in the Declaration of Quebec City, an unconstitutional interruption of the democratic order or an unconstitutional alteration of the constitutional regime that seriously impairs the democratic order in a member state, constitutes, while it persists, an insurmountable obstacle to its government's participation in sessions of the General Assembly, the Meeting of Consultation, the Councils of the Organization, the specialized conferences, the commissions, working groups, and other bodies of the Organization.

In the event of an unconstitutional alteration of the constitutional regime that seriously impairs the democratic order in a member state, any member state or the Secretary General may request the immediate convocation of the Permanent Council to undertake a collective assessment of the situation and to take such decisions as it deems appropriate. The Permanent Council, depending on the situation, may undertake the necessary diplomatic initiatives, including good offices, to foster the restoration of democracy.

If such diplomatic initiatives prove unsuccessful, or if the urgency of the situation so warrants, the Permanent Council shall immediately convene a special session of the General Assembly. The General Assembly will adopt the decisions it deems appropriate, including the undertaking of diplomatic initiatives, in accordance with the Charter of the Organization, international law, and the provisions of this Democratic Charter.

The necessary diplomatic initiatives, including good offices, to foster the restoration of democracy, will continue during the process

Pursuant to stipulations derived from the OAS, when a member State violates the democratic institutionalism that sustains its political system, shall be impeded from participating in the General Assembly, the Meeting of Consultation, the Councils of the Organization and the specialized conferences, as well as the commissions, working groups and other bodies of the Organization. It guarantees an immediate sanction to those States that stay apart from the democratic system. In addition, having verified the violation of the democratic order, any member State or the Secretary General shall have the authority to convoke the Permanent Council to undertake a joint assessment of the facts and, therefore, implement the actions it deems necessary to reinsert it in the democratic nations system. The Permanent Council, by diplomatic initiatives, shall foster the restoration of democratic stability.

Suspension of infringing state

> When the special session of the General Assembly determines that there has been an unconstitutional interruption of the democratic order of a member state, and that diplomatic initiatives have failed, the special session shall take the decision to suspend said member state from the exercise of its right to participate in the OAS by an affirmative vote of two thirds of the member states in accordance with the Charter of the OAS. The suspension shall take effect immediately.
>
> The suspended member state shall continue to fulfill its obligations to the Organization, in particular its human rights obligations.
>
> Notwithstanding the suspension of the member state, the Organization will maintain diplomatic initiatives to restore democracy in that state (article 21).

As we have stated, one of the risks that threatens stability of the Latin American nations is the eventual interruption of the constitutional order as a result of a coup d'etat. Once it has been verified that the democratic order in a state has been interrupted, such member state will be suspended from participating in the OAS. Despite such suspension, that state shall not be exempted to fulfill its obligations in human rights field and, in spite of being in force the suspension, the diplomatic initiatives to restore that state in the lost democratic scope, shall continue. This suspension is a direct legacy from the named «Betancourt Doctrine» that we will revise in later topics.

Lift of the suspension

The Inter American Democratic Charter stipulates that:

> Once the situation that led to suspension has been resolved, any member state or the Secretary General may propose to the General Assembly that suspension be lifted. This decision shall require the vote of two thirds of the member states in accordance with the OAS Charter (article 22).

It is a process in which a suspended government may be reinserted in the OAS, after the reason of suspension has ceased. We consider that, despite it is stated in the Charter the suspension of a state, it is the infringing government the one that is suspended. In most cases, the lift of the suspension proceeds when the government that has denied a live in democracy is substituted by a regime of political, social and economic liberties.

Democracy and Electoral Observation Missions

> Member states are responsible for organizing, conducting, and ensuring free and fair electoral processes.
>
> Member states, in the exercise of their sovereignty, may request that the Organization of American States provide advisory services or assistance for strengthening and developing their electoral institutions and processes, including sending preliminary missions for that purpose.
>
> The electoral observation missions shall be carried out at the request of the member state concerned. To that end, the government of that state and the Secretary General shall enter into an agreement establishing the scope and coverage of the electoral observation mission in question. The member state shall guarantee conditions of security, free access to information, and full cooperation with the electoral observation mission.
>
> Electoral observation missions shall be carried out in accordance with the principles and norms of the OAS. The Organization shall ensure that these missions are effective and independent and shall provide them with the necessary resources for that purpose. They shall be conducted in an objective, impartial, and transparent manner and with the appropriate technical expertise.
>
> Electoral observation missions shall present a report on their activities in a timely manner to the Permanent Council, through the General Secretariat (articles 23 and 24).

The named electoral watchers of the OAS have a fundamental mission in this process. They will observe its integrity, issue a report related to the compliance of the peoples willingness and watch for it not being disturbed by those who control the authority of the state.

Electoral observation

> The electoral observation missions shall advise the Permanent Council, through the General Secretariat, if the necessary conditions for free and fair elections do not exist (article 25).

In case observers consider the lack of the necessary conditions for elections, they shall inform the Permanent Council, which may initiate as deemed necessary to contribute for the creation of the required conditions.

Promotion of democratic culture

The OAS will continue to carry out programs and activities designed to promote democratic principles and practices and strengthen a democratic culture in the Hemisphere, bearing in mind that democracy is a way of life based on liberty and enhancement of economic, social, and cultural conditions for the peoples of the Americas. The OAS will consult and cooperate on an ongoing basis with member states and take into account the contributions of civil society organizations working in those fields.

The objectives of the programs and activities will be to promote good governance, sound administration, democratic values, and the strengthening of political institutions and civil society organizations. Special attention shall be given to the development of programs and activities for the education of children and youth as a means of ensuring the continuance of democratic values, including liberty and social justice.

States shall promote the full and equal participation of women in the political structures of their countries as a fundamental element in the promotion and exercise of a democratic culture (articles 26, 27 and 28).

Democratic culture is not a fact. It is an intro-culturization to insert a community in a democratic life, on the basis of cognitive processes that be reflected in the values of liberty transmitted by democratic action. It will impact not only in the cultural process of social and political identification, but also in the relation government/society, as of high scores of governability.

CHAPTER V

THE INTERNATIONAL COMMUNITY

The International Community in XXI century: the hegemonic global state and some considerations of the beginning of century. Evolution of the international community. United Nations. Charter of the UN: purposes, principles and organization. Organization of American States: purposes, principles, organs and roles. Other conceptions of Law: Islamic Law. The world order of the future: unipolar or multipolar?

The Law must command, not argue

Seneca

THE INTERNATIONAL COMMUNITY IN THE XXI CENTURY: THE HEGEMONIC GLOBAL STATE AND SOME CONSIDERATIONS OF THE BEGINNING OF THE CENTURY

Because of recent events, which by the time this chapter was written had the attention of the world -the war against terrorism started by the United States as of the events of September 11th, when it was object of attack allegedly planned by the terrorist red Al Qaeda, and the war in Iraq, which ended with the defeating of Saddam Hussein-, we face a question: is the international system reorganizing itself towards a change, or has the United States started the implementation of American peace, determined to conduct a change in the system? In one way or the other, it seems that with these facts Public International Law has no much to do or not enough strength is left, taking into consideration that the power of the States, with the capacity to exercise it, overtakes the authority of law, the principles and treaties from which they are derived.

XX century represented the victory of technology over intra and international violence. Despite technological development made possible the war to move forward at a higher scale, it also put an end to it and warned human being about the imminent risk of its disappearance whether rationality did not impose over in regards of peace. Cold war, which defined the equilibrium of power in the international structure, constituted itself in a «panacea» that allowed nations to live in apparent peace, while the great powers, among threatens and treaties on regulation of weapons, sought to extend the scope of political and social influence.

To some authors, such as Fukuyama (1992), the fall of the Berlin Wall meant the end of history, the victory of liberalism and democracies; others, such as Samuel Huntington, focused on the new world order defined by ethnical and cultural conflicts. The traditional realist conceptions of Morgenthau (1963), Kennan (1952) and others were sustained to them, who explained the international battle as of interest-power formula. It means that all nations based their international policies in the pursuit of power to satisfy its national interests. Today it seems that the realist paradigm expresses its enforcement when we approach to the phenomenon of war.

The history is clear at explaining the evolution of the international structure of XX century. Four international systems are revised by Pearson and Rochester (2000): classic system (1648-1789), transition (1789-1945), after World War II (1945-1989) and contemporary (1989-2000). On the other hand, there are lots of historical and political studies that analyze the evolution of the international structure and give every system a specific characteristic, where it is agreed to identify the existence of Nation-state. Studies posted on the second half of XX century arisen concepts such as Region-state and Nucleon-state (Kaldor, 2001) which explain the extension of power and the influence of national states.

When the first war of XXI century starts, in which the USA, under a Kantian excuse of freedom, protects its national security from eventual terrorist attacks driven by individual factors linked to Iraq and Al Qaeda, and the criticism of those who affirm that it is a war for oil, it is evident there is a realistic content in the act. This global war seeks for reaffirming the USA scope of influence, its hegemonic character in the western hemisphere and the global expansion of the political, economic and social power. So, the concept of hegemonic global state emerges, according to which a military, political, economic and social powerful country may impose over the rest of them to develop a world government model.

This represents the highest expression of the exercise of power to impose not only an easily influenced political model, but also a culture aim to drive the change of the political map in the Middle East. Therefore, the fight for absolute power in XXI century, under the framework of «Bush Doctrine», puts aside the influence of diplomacy and imposes the strength violating the regulations of Public International Law, which afterwards will not be an obstacle for the reconfiguration of a structured new world order, headed by the state that gets all the power.

The aforesaid leads to a valuable consideration: there are different definitions for international society in regards of the conceptual approximation that may be made of it. It suggests the valuable sociocultural impact to identify the type of international society we have, full of ethnic diversity, versus the western acceptation that imposed its Christian values to conceive the political structure of the United Nations Organization which, from a defensive and secure framework, has moved forward to a inclusion and integration one.

So, some authors such as Monroy Cabra distinguish the concepts of international society and international community. The latter is defined as «a set of collective entities relating each other by regulations of Public International Law» (1998:301), while the former is constituted in the social base of the international community in the «specific/concrete social creation/formation that is the foundation of the coexistence background of the peoples and persons in the history of humankind [...] without being limited to the regulation of sovereign states, and also understanding the interstate organization and other entities» *(Ibid)*.

In order to understand the social-political structure of the international community and the international society, we have to review the factual evolution of the cotemporary international community. This historical-political review, instead of being a limited academic element, shall ease the comprehension of the late changes occurred since the events of 9/11 in New York.

EVOLUTION OF THE INTERNATIONAL COMMUNITY

We have to bear in mind that in Chapter I we quoted the evolution of International Law in the context of the variations occurred in the international community. To speak only about the historiographical and chronological process, as we have done, would make us sound redundant regarding topics already analyzed. On the contrary, the formal focus of structures that existed to bring new frameworks may make us understand the rational and legal use to which our work is oriented.

We consider approaching the process of change and evolution as the cornerstone, beginning with two elements: a social one and a bureaucratic-political one. This put us on the «cultural values» versus «real power» dichotomy. Cultural values are defined by a sociologic impact, while real power is summarized as the real or potential capacity that a Nation-state has to impose political or economically over the rest.

We will recapture the speech regarding the final consideration that will pertain to the definition of the new world order or in transition order: military unipolar or economic multipolar. On this matter, the structure of our approach will be limited to review the defining factors and characteristics of the international community construct, by the end of XIX century until the constitution of the League of Nations.

Elements and features of the Western European World

The idea of progress, the reason, science and ideology as political and Law instruments are defining elements of the historical process between 1894 and 1914. Before the Great War in Europe, in 1914, the European society was sustained over the values and ideals generated by the Scientific Revolution and Illustration. On one hand, science strengthened its reputation as a result of the invention of the electric light, the phonograph and the automobile. On the other, a legal transformation with social influence defined European relations in XIX century: Women's rights movements.

...Truthfully, the main objective of the Congress of Vienna was to restructure the European map, after Napoleon was defeated, with the purpose of achieving peace maintenance, the establishment of a new European system; that is, a new world order, which rules of procedure made possible a relative peace in Europe for one hundred years.

As the Quadruple Alliance was reaffirmed, composed of Great Britain, Russia, Prussia and Austria, the compromise to fights against any attempt to set up the Bonaparte's regime (Spielvogel, 1997:741) was renewed, and the four periodic conferences that took place between 1818 and 1822, were established. That is, Aix-la-Chapelle, 1818; Troppau, 1820; Laibach, 1821; and Verone, 1822. Troppau is the most important conference in Public International Law matters to be herein studied, in which the principle of non-intervention[23] was proposed.

The conservative order imposed since 1815 neither could stop the influence of liberalism and revolutionary ideas held between 1820 and 1830, nor the wars that were held between 1854 and 1871[24] The new imperialism established in 1880 defined the subordinate role of International Law as of real power of the states. Then, early that year, European states were in war, encouraged by expansionist needs. This new imperialism led European states to distribute each other the Asian and African continents.

The development of technology defined the reasons as for I World War took place. In fact, with the Great War in 1914, the equilibrium of power was overthrown, which, as said before, had kept peace in Europe for a hundred

---

23 According to Spielvogel, the document in which the principle is stipulated, stated that «if a State were to be found threatened by disruptive elements, the great powers were obliged by peaceful mechanisms or weapons to return the guilty state to the framework of Quadruple Alliance» (1997:737-744).

24 We are referring to Crimea War, Danish War, Austro-Prussian War and Franco-Prussian War.

years. The principle of equilibrium of power established an acknowledged rule of international custom, in which all nations headed their policies to avoid them from achieving an outstanding/predominant position that allowed them be over the others, In regards of the foundation of equilibrium of power, Public International Law would get independence in terms of maintenance of an international legal order of equality among states, which would only be broken with opening hostilities.

Reference to the League of Nations

The League of Nations, created by virtue of the need to maintain peace through the construction of an international order, was the name given due to the 14 Points proposed by President Woodrow Wilson, enumerated in a message given in front the Congress, on January 8th 1918. The purpose of these proposals was to set the boundaries of a just and lasting peace after World War I. Point number 14 of Wilson was what, finally, turned out in the named League of Nations, as a result of the Paris Peace Conference, 1919.

The idealism expressed in the aforesaid proposals was highly supported and provided Wilson a moral leadership position in the Peace Conference. However, by the end of the war, European allies were against to some of the points, and the attempt to put in practice the 14 Points, prompted a multilateral system of secret agreements among the defeated ones. In order to achieve the necessary support for Point number 14 -the most important of all in which it was required the creation of a general association of nations-. Wilson felt forced to give up on the approval of his program. The 14 Points were as follows:

1. There shall be no private international understandings of any kind but diplomacy shall proceed always frankly and in the public view.

2. Absolute freedom of navigation upon the seas, outside territorial waters, alike in peace and in war, except as the seas may be closed in whole or in part by international action for the enforcement of international covenants.

3. The removal, so far as possible, of all economic barriers and the establishment of an equality of trade conditions among all the nations consenting to the peace and associating themselves for its maintenance.

4. Adequate guarantees given and taken that national armaments will be reduced to the lowest point consistent with domestic safety.

5. An adjustment of all colonial claims, based upon a strict observance of the principle that in determining all such questions of sovereignty the interests of the populations concerned must have equal weight with the equitable claims of the government whose title is to be determined.

6. The evacuation of all Russian territory, guaranteeing its autonomy.
7. Belgium, the whole world will agree, must be evacuated and restored.
8. All French territory should be freed and the invaded portions restored, including Alsace and Lorraine.
9. A readjustment of the frontiers of Italy should be effected along clearly recognizable lines of nationality.
10. The autonomy for nationalities existing in Austria and Hungary.
11. The evacuation of Rumania, Serbia, and Montenegro, guaranteeing Serbia free and secure access to the sea, and international protection to Balkan states nationalist claims
12. Independence of non-Turkish peoples of the Ottoman Empire and internationalization of the Dardanelles.
13. The creation of an independent Polish state with access to the sea.
14. The creation of a general association of nations under specific covenants for the purpose of affording mutual guarantees of political independence and territorial integrity.

The normative pact that created the League of Nations, constituted by 26 articles, expressed the commitment among the signatory states not to open a war, to maintain the rules of international relations founded in justice and honor, to vigorously watch for the fundamental norms of International Law and to respect the obligations agreed upon the treaties. The main purpose was to set the spirit of cooperation among the nations to guarantee them peace and security[25] The organization and functioning of the League of Nations was set up into two complementary directions: the guarantee of peace through collective security and the building of peace through cooperation.

The collective security system, which enrooted the political dimension of society, was stipulated in articles 8 to 17. Those articles stated the regulation of legal and political system guidance on the prevention of war, in which different principles interacted: the guarantee of integrity of the territory and the independence of National states, collective assistance, arbitration, setting of boundaries of Law in the use of violence and a system of sanctions. The aforesaid system was founded in a triplet: arbitration, disarmament and security. To guarantee and maintain peace and security required, the adoption of a solidarity system and international cooperation, and to such effect articles 23 to 25 were arisen. International cooperation expressed the conviction of peace being possible if social justice was provided,

25 This realistic statement contradicted the idealist conduct that proved the weakness of the actions taken against the nations that threatened against peace.

through the promotion of mutual assistance on economic, cultural and humanitarian matters[26].

In regards of the aforesaid principles an institutional structure was stipulated, upraising the scope of the new international organization. The new international management had a group of central organs; two of them have a political and interstate nature: the Council and the Assembly (articles 3 to 5), which shall rule all matters involved in the Society range of activity or might affect world peace. The Council, which would end up as an Executive Committee, created in the midst of 1920, and was convoked at least three times a year, and within its framework his permanent members deliberated: France, Great Britain, Italy and Japan. Furthermore, Germany, the Soviet Union and other temporary members were added, as well as those chosen as semi-permanent members.

The General Assembly was the democratic organ of the League of Nations, which celebrated a regular meeting in September. The Permanent Secretary was basically a technical-administrative organ which was founded pursuant to provisions of article 2. Sir Eric Drummond, an experienced English diplomat, was appointed as first Secretary General (Spielvogel, 1997). The institutional complexity had a set of subsidiary organs of the system, both political and technical, and also a set of autonomous organs linked to the League of Nations, such as the Permanent Court of International Justice, created in 1921, which seat was established in The Hague, Netherlands; and the International Labour Organization, founded in 1919.

Despite most leaders and diplomats' good will, the League of Nations, created by the Geneva Conventions[27], did not have the right conditions to solemnize equal commitments, nor maintain the established order. The shyness of its performance to prevent Abyssinia from being conquered proved the weakness of its power. That was reaffirmed as the expansionist policy of the fascist powers in Europe, which resulted in the opening of the World War II, could not be controlled.

THE UNITED NATIONS. UN CHARTER: PURPOSES, PRINCIPLES AND ORGANIZATION.

The United Nations Organization (UNO) is the heir of the League of Nations. It is an international organization of Nation-states founded in the principle of sovereign equality. Pursuant to the foundational charter, which

26 Nowadays it seems the weaknesses in which the League of Nations incurred, trespass the collaborative spirit of the UN, which we will study in this chapter and will lead us think about the ideas expressed at the beginning of this topic, regarding the upcoming of the hegemonic global state.

27 See Chapter I.

entered in force on October 24th 1945, the UN was established to «maintain international peace and security», «to develop friendly relations among nations», «to achieve international co-operation in solving international problems of an economic, social, cultural, or humanitarian character» and «to promote respect for human rights and for fundamental freedoms».

Some of the commitments established by the Member states were to fulfill the obligations assumed and settle international disputes by peaceful means, refraining from the threat or use of force. In addition, they are obliged to assist in any organized actions in accordance with the Charter and not to assist to any State against which the UN is taking actions.

As a primary background of the United Nations Organization, the Atlantic Charter is acknowledged, which was signed by American President Franklin Delano Roosevelt y British Prime Minister Winton Churchill, on August 14th 1941, in a conference celebrated aboard of a war ship in front of the Terranova Coasts. Both leaders agreed to establish a «permanent and wider system of general security» and expressed their desire «to achieve full collaboration from all nations on economic matters». The Atlantic Charter foundations were accepted by all allied nations in a firmer manner in its Declaration. It was in that declaration in which, for the first time, the official name of «United Nations» was used and had been proposed by President Roosevelt.

In 1943, during World War II, a conference was celebrated in Moscow, in which procedures were started to create a new international structure. On October 30th 1943, representatives of the Soviet Union, United Kingdom, China and the United States signed a treaty in which it was acknowledged the necessity «to establish in short period of time a general international organization». Furthermore, in a meeting celebrated in Tehran (Iran), Roosevelt, Churchill and Stalin created «the supreme responsibility that relies on us and all the United Nations to achieve a peace that banishes the sorrow and terror of war».

After the Moscow treaty, representatives of the four allied powers met in Dumbarton Oaks, Washington, in 1994, to review a number of proposals oriented to create an international organization. It was approved a first draft stating tis purposes, structures and operational mechanisms, but no agreement was made regarding the election of the Security Council already proposed, which would end up being the body with major responsibility on peace maintenance and protection matters, as well as collective security. Afterwards, the Charter of the United Nations was approved in a final draft. It stipulates six principal organs: the General Assembly, the Security Council, the Economic and Social Council, the Trusteeship Council, the International Court of Justice and the General Secretariat.

Principal organs: functions. Principal members: duties and rights.

All Member states will be represented in the General Assembly, which is the principal deliberation organ of the Organization. That is annually met in ordinary sessions and special sessions upon request of the majority of its members or the Security Council. It has no power to make its resolutions being complied with, as they are just mere recommendations given to Member states. The Charter allows the General Assembly to establish agencies and programs that performance its recommendations. The most important ones include: the United Nations Development Program (UNDP), United Nations Conference on Trade and Development (Unctad) and the United Nations Children's Fund (UNICEF).

The Security Council

It is the central and permanent organ for peace maintenance. It consists of 15 members, five of them are permanent: China, France, United Kingdom, Russia and United States. Non-permanent members are elected for a two-year-period, and the General Assembly elects five new members each year. Nine votes are necessary to pass the Council's decisions, including all of the permanent members in regards to great importance matters.

The Economic and Social Council

It has an annual meeting and consists of 54 members, 18 of them are elected once a year by the General Assembly to exercise a triennial mandate. In addition to this, it also coordinates the economic and social activities of the UN and its specialized agencies, including the World Health Organization (WHO), UNESCO, Food and Agriculture Organization of the United Nations (FAO) and the International Labor Organization (ILO). In practice, it has limited functions since each specialized agency is organized independently and ruled by its own bylaws and election organs. Those agencies issue annual reports to the Economic Council.

The Trusteeship Council

At the beginning its responsibility relied on the supervision of 11 territories under the regime of trust at the end of World War II. Later on, in the 90's, all trustee territories which had been under international supervision, had reached absolute independence or its autonomy under the basis of a state. Palau Islands was maintained as trustee, which became the Independent Republic of Palau in 1994; therefore, the Trusteeship Council entered into a process of disappearance. Other related colonial matters have been transferred to the General Assembly and special subsidiary organs.

The International Court of Justice

It is located in The Hague, Netherlands. It is the main judicial organ of the UN and deals with cases transferred by members of the UN. In addition, it shall have advisory opinion. It consists of 15 judges, elected by the General Assembly and the Security Council, for a nine-year-term. In a legal scope, to this court was also added the International Criminal Court, which bylaws were approved in 1998 and is in charge of the prosecution of individuals who committed «the worst crimes against the international community».

It is important to point out that the greatest power of the world, United States, currently holds the military hegemonic power, and has refused to be part of the International Criminal Court due to the actions taken (overseas) by their troops to maintain peace or comply with the American Foreign Policy objectives. This situation makes us consider about the weakness of such organ in regards of the eventual coercive power to prosecute American criminals of war, in the case certain boundaries were crossed, committed against societies.

The General Secretariat

It shall be at the service of the rest organs of the UN and implement the programs and policies of the Organization. The Secretariat is represented by the Secretary General, appointed by the General Assembly upon recommendation of the Security Council. Since the UN was founded, it has had seven Secretaries General: Trygve Halvdan Lie (1946-1953), Dag Hjalmar Hammarskjold (1953-1961), Sithu U Thant (1961-1971), Kurt Waldheim (1972-1981), Javier Perez de Cuellar (1982-1991), Butros Butros-Gali (1992-1996) and Kofi Annan, Ban Ki-moon (2007-2016) and the current Secretary General Antonio Guterres

THE ORGANIZATION OF AMERICAN STATES: PURPOSES, PRINIPLES, ORGANS AND FUNCTIONS.

The Organization of American States is a supranational organization within a regional scope, consisted of all states of the American continent, except for Cuba that was expelled upon request of the Government of Venezuela, ruled at that time by President Romulo Betancourt. The Organization was founded by the 21 countries that, on April 30th 1948, during the IX Pan-American Conference, adopted the Pact of Bogota. Such Pact created the American Treaty on Pacific Settlement, signed in Bogota, on April 30th 1948, by the governments represented at the IX Pan-American Conference. It entered into force on May 6th 1949.

The OAS was born in the Pan-American framework. Its immediate background was the International Union of American Republics (called Pan-American Union in 1910), founded in 1890 and was to become the Secretariat General in 1948. The OAS main purposes, as stated in its bylaws, are as follows:

1. To strengthen the peace and security of the continent.
2. To promote and consolidate representative democracy, with due respect for the principle of nonintervention.

3. To prevent possible causes of difficulties and to ensure the pacific settlement of disputes that may arise among the Member States.
4. To provide for common action on the part of those States in the event of aggression.
5. To seek the solution of political, juridical, and economic problems that may arise among them.
6. To promote, by cooperative action, their economic, social, and cultural development.
7. To achieve an effective limitation of conventional weapons that will make it possible to devote the largest amount of resources to the economic and social development of the Member States.

The OAS foundational Charter has been amended on four occasions: by the Protocol of Buenos Aires, signed in 1967 and entered into force in 1970; the Protocol of Cartagena de Indias, signed in 1985 and entered into force in 1988; the Protocol Washington, signed in 1992 and entered into force in 1997; and the Protocol of Managua; the Charter of Quebec and the Democratic Charter, recently created. These bylaws amendments were made for the following purposes: to achieve a better integration and economic development among the nations of the hemisphere, to promote and defend representative democracies, to help overcome poverty, and to achieve a better use of supplies of technical cooperation.

The principal organs of the OAS include: the General Assembly, The Meeting of Consultation of Ministers of Foreign Affairs, the Permanent Council and the General Secretariat. As for its specialized organizations, it includes: the Inter-American Council for Education, Science and Culture (ICESC), the Inter-American Economic and Social Council (IESC), the Inter-American Juridical Committee (IJC), the Inter-American Commission on Human Rights (ICHR), the Inter-American Indigenous Institute (III) and the Pan-American Health Organization (PHO). After the Protocol of Managua was ratified, the Inter-American Council for Integral Development (ICID) replaced the former IESC and ICESC.

The Secretary General, highest responsible of the General Secretariat, is elected by the General Assembly for a five-year-term and cannot be reelected for more than two consecutive terms[28]. On the other hand, the founder Members of the OAS include: Argentina, Bolivia, Brazil, Chile, Colombia, Costa Rica, Cuba, Dominican Republic, Ecuador, El Salvador, Guatemala, Haiti, Honduras, Mexico, Nicaragua, Panama, Paraguay, Peru, United States, Uruguay and

---

[28] On Monday, May 2nd 2005, the new Secretary General of the OAS was appointed in Washington, the former Chilean Minister of Interior, Jose Miguel Insulza.

Venezuela. Afterwards, Barbados (1967), Trinidad and Tobago (19670, Jamaica (1969), Grenada (1975), Surinam (1977), Dominica (1979), Saint Lucia (1979), Antigua and Barbuda (1981), Saint Vincent and the Grenadines (1981), Bahamas (1982), Saint Kitts and Nevis (1984), Canada (1990), Belize (1991) and Guyana (1991) acquired the status of Member states.

OTHER CONCEPTIONS OF LAW: ISLAMIC LAW

Why should we study the fundamental elements of Islamic Law in this chapter? The response underlies on the principle of inclusion. As we have seen before, the United Nations have conceived the world order from an ethnocentric and western perspective, excluding Islamic nations or, at least, their point of view towards the world and law. It deems necessary to review foundations of Public International Law when it comes to provide it with new definitions, since this exclusion may, direct or indirectly, be the beginning of the end of the new world order, achieved peace and the power of the Western. A new war may help us understand, from a realistic perspective but humanitarian, the real sense of the principle of inclusion as fundamental element of international security.

As appointed by the doctrine, the first systematic inquiries of the Islamic legislation were found in a file of texts granted to specialists in late VIII and early IX centuries, in which we include: Abu Hanifa, Malik, Shafi'I and Ahmad Ibn Hanbal, the four magnets of the Sunni community. Each one of them is considered founder of a juridical school named *Madhab*. Those four schools, bonded by the legal tradition of *shiism*, the other principal branch of if Islam, represent the five most relevant Islamic juridical sources.

According to Muslim creed, Prophet Muhammad served as role model for his community. When he passed away, in 632, he left the *Coram* as principal foundation of law, along with the *Sunna,* which was transferred from generations to generations as narrations, known as the *Hadit.* Eventually, the Hadit derived arguments, analysis and, finally, legal formal discussions, all collected in masterpieces of the four magnets.

That description of the origin of Islamic Law was criticized by western specialists. According to them, what actually reflects the first masterpieces of Islamic Law are the own traditions of the communities of Kufa, Medina and Damascus. Such traditions are based on the local practice and were vaguely related to the idea of prophetic *Sunna.* Well, from a juridical research point of view, there are 2 main categories in Islamic legal literature: the *furu'al-fiqh* (branches of law) and the *usul al-fiqh* (roots of law). The former consists of a set of rules thematically organized. A piece of *furu'* always suggests, first of all, worship and relations of man with God *('ibadat),* that is, about the pureness, prayer, charity, fasting and pilgrimage, and on occasions also it was referring to the Holy War. The rest of text, named *ibadat,* or regulation of man's behavior with their similars, it expresses legal aspects of a treaty of marriage, divorce, inheritance, sanctions for assaults, murder and illegal assumption of goods; sales, representation and labor contracts; other social matters, such as dress, hygiene and nutrition codes. The masterpieces of furu had several purposes: educational, aesthetical, theological, and strictly legal. They were not as much legal manuscripts but considerations about law.

The compliance of Divine Law in the community depended on three officers, each one with its own functions: the *cadi* or judge, the *mufti* or law specialist and the *alfaqui*. The cadi was appointed by the Governor and his mission consisted of being the judge in a lawsuit and to watch for certain matters affecting the community, such as those related to orphan's goods and trusts management. This function of administration of justice, with a practical character and unavoidable social implications, was necessary, but it was exposed to corruptive conducts and represented a threatening to individual salvation.

The *mufi* was part of a higher scale. Its function was to offer conclusive responses to inquires made by the peoples regarding the law. However, his decisions were official and did not comply as the ones issued by the judge. Finally, the position of the *alfaqui* had the highest honor and range. His labor consisted of analyzing the law in regards of revelation and the tradition of the School. He had the power to express his preferences, but to not express the law wrongly. Since he was dedicated to study the tradition, his scope of action was not related to practical legal matters. (Robinson, 1994)

THE WORLD ORDER OF THE FUTURE: UNIPOLAR OR MULTIPOLAR?

Been revised the international community in its fundamental institutions, through the political changes of history and its legal impact, we have to think about this enquiry: How is and will the world order in construction be? Unpretentiously attempting to predict or judge the process of change, we consider the existence of four scenarios that could explain the upcoming world order. First of all, we have a peace order under the hegemonic supremacy of the defeater of Cold War, statement in which we started this chapter. Second, we have a later war order, as a result of the weakness of law. Third, there is a peace order, under the power of Law, in the hands of the congregated nations in an Organization capable of not committing the errors committed in the League of Nations and commit the United Nations Organization. Finally, there is an order tending to a global conflict, as a consequence of intolerance, the abuse of military power and the increase of terrorism in the world.

CHAPTER VI

FOREIGN POLICY AND INTERNATIONAL LAW

Foreign Policy. Political systems and Public International Law

«If the foundation is taken, the pact is suppressed»

Spinoza

FOREIGN POLICY

Concept

There are many concepts of foreign policy that have been produced in the XX century and for many decades. This has undoubtedly resulted from investigations that have brought intellectual leaders together in order to find the most accurate definition. On our end, as a contribution to these efforts and basing our approach in each one of the variables that have had an influence on its construction, we have come up with a concept: the foreign policy of a Nation-state is a rational construction of public policy that contains planned public actions or improvised reactions that are stimulated by the international structure, by international organizations or by Nation-states with real power. These actions are developed from topics, tendencies and interests that are related to the political-ideological model designed by the national project and the government's political program.

Nonetheless, we know previous researchers have developed a more accurate definition than the one we present now. Pearson and Rochester (2000), who believe that foreign policy is «a set of priorities or stipulated by the national leaders to act as a series of behaviors in different courses of action, in specific situations and within the context in which they struggle to achieve goals' (p 197). Marcel Merle (1966) defines foreign policy as the art to manage the relations of one State with the other States. Maria Teresa Romero (2002) suggests foreign policy is part of the general policy of a Nation-state as one of the dimensions of political action taken by such State.

Elsa Cardozo Da Silva (2001) states that foreign policy is the one that is to be formulated and developed by the government and connects us with the rest of the world. Finally, Yoston Ferrigni, Carlos Gueron and Eva Josko de Gueron (1984) agree on defining foreign policy as the process that displays different solutions found by the State to the claims originated from its domestic nature as well as its national system and its role as international player.

Foreign policy uses the means available to widely respond to the national claims, for every foreign policy is a part of the national system in which the people responsible for making decisions have to evaluate the different means coming from their power potential in order to face an international system and choose their goals in such a manner it is not contradictory with the national plans. This explains why foreign policy is a process that depends on or it is in permanent change contingent on the development of internal variables such as the national political system and international variables such as the international structure. Louis Henkin (1979) says foreign policy is a sum of all attitudes reflected in the numerous points of contact a nation as with others, big or small.

In order to better develop the previous concepts, it is necessary to revise them in the light of international relations. On one hand, the national interests are a key factor managed by the pupils of the Political Realism to analyze foreign policy. Its content verses on the traditional policies and the cultural context of each nation. They assure the national interest is part of the formulation of both the internal and the external policy. Stanley Hoffman (1979) - another realist - says the precise definition of national interest enables the orientation, objectives and actions of the foreign policy of a State.

All the statists have to have a relatively uniform idea of the meaning of national interest. This can be achieved by evaluating each of the demands of the sectors of the State. The addition of economic, political, social, union pressures and others constitute the national interest. Another element that adds to the notion of national interest is the concept of security that entails the protection of the sovereignty and independence, the integrity of the territory and the country's people's lives. Besides, Merle (1966) introduces the essence of foreign policy by identifying a third element related to the national interest and manifested in its policy of cooperation and development, which would be advantageous by performing a clever diplomacy, capable of opening new markets that can be profitable for exporting national products.

Yet, the national interest is not an ethical duty, which shows some inconsistency between the political ethics and the concepts of national interest and power. Morgenthau (1963) refers to two elements that are part of the national interest:

1. Any foreign policy aligned with the national interest should refer to the physical, political and cultural entity we call a nation.

2. In a world in which nations and countries compete and fight for power, foreign policy should respond to the survival of the State as a minimum requirement. Hence, all countries design their policies in order to protect their physical, political and cultural identity.

Most of the authors agree on stating that the national interest changes with the demands derived from the international structure; therefore it is a dynamic concept that tailors the needs of ideological, cultural, material, religious and strategic factors. Elsa Cardozo says it is necessary to perform a regular revision of the content of the national interest and even «to redefine it if required by the political circumstances» (2001: 11).

Venezuelan Foreign Policy: general theoretical aspects

The next pages will show an analysis of the theory and methods of study of the foreign policy in Venezuela within the context of the history of the Venezuelan political system. We will study how the methods and theory provide a better understanding of the political phenomena and in the formulation of foreign policy. We believe it is useful to understand how the systems theory, the focus on the agenda and the realist paradigm can offer a closer approach to study cases in foreign policy as well as public policy both in a specific and a more general context.

The political party system background is a part of the birth of the contemporary system of foreign policy. The policies implemented in the governments of Perez Jimenez, Betancourt and Caldera are the cornerstone for the process of foreign policy, based on two premises: The changes that produced the events on January 23rd, 1958 which also became a valuable element in the political system that was later established; and the political momentum reflected on the change of power from one political factor to another one within the democracy, but with bureaucratic and ideological variations that had an influence on the domestic political scheme and did not perturb the development to a much better definition of democracy.

To explore the problems of study of Venezuela's foreign policy is an intellectual task of scientific nature that leads us to evaluate the importance of theoretical (paradigmatic) and historical elements that can explain the phenomena from a perspective free from the subjective elements that often have an influence on the analysis. Based on this premise, a question comes up: What is a Nation-state's foreign policy and what is it for? Yet, before we produce our own definition, we find it necessary to verify what has been written on the matter, based on different methodological and paradigmatic approaches, like the history involved in this process.

Yoston Ferrigni, Carlos Gueron and Eva Josko de Gueron, from a systemic approach, state that «a Nation-state is a dialectic process of objectives-means-action and results» (1984: 80). Such process got the Nation-state involved with the international system in another process that can be explained with the «systems theory», which was incorporated into the social sciences by David Easton (1992), Gabriel Almond (1986), Karl Deutsch (1974), and Talcot Parson[29].

According to Easton, the systems theory is based on «the idea of the political life being a set of interactions within certain boundaries which is inserted and surrounded by other social systems that constantly influence it» (Dougherty and Plaltzgraff, 1990: 157). The political interactions can be fundamentally differentiated from the others by the fact that they are oriented toward the authoritarian distribution of values in a society; that is to say, an imposition of values.

The use Ferrigni, Gueron and Josko (Ibid) make of the systemic approach leads them to consider there is an interaction between domestic and international which establishes a balance in the national system inputs which simultaneously operates as an output for the international system. The objectives-means-action and results scheme is useful to show a piece of the process of political action but it does not take the intellectual motivation for the definition of the objectives into consideration; that is to say, it does not consider the rational or irrational condition of the decision-making process. They certainly warn about this in their paper. However, for the sake of this topic, we believe this is an element of judge and it is indispensable for the study of Venezuela's foreign policy.

In our view, we find the objectives-means-action and results scheme appropriate as an element to evaluate the political process. The objectives are determined by the orientation (rational or irrational) of the desired end (permanent or temporary objectives and interests). The means are part of the actual capability or the potential a national role player has to take the political action forward and has the skills to evaluate the results.

Ferrigni, Gueron and Josko (Ibid) revisit the variables Gabriel Almond (1986) identifies as the inputs that feed the political system: political socialization, political recruitment, interest, articulation of interests, inclusion of interests, and political communication. The outputs are the role of the government in the decision-making process. All these variables add to the process that comes from the international system which also feeds the political system and transforms the elements of influence in inputs.

Every foreign policy is public policy because it is created by the State, and it should contain the interests of the community, which can be affected in different degrees, depending on the results derived from such policy. Besides, The State's public policy in a given sector aims for the creation of «conditions

29 «Systems theory». In Dougherry and Platzgraff (1991). International Relations Theories in Conflict. Buenos Aires: Grupo Editor Latinoamericano, p. 176.

for a specific situation to be produced or for certain activities to be displayed and performed» (Njaim, 1978: 1). This is determined by a theoretical construction that helps understand the consistency and repetition of behaviors associated with the efforts of the State to resolve problems of public nature. The context in which an agenda of public policies for foreign affairs is performed may be perceived as extremely complex. This makes it difficult to clearly understand the results and effects related to each option, as well as to anticipate all of the implications and its consequences. Therefore, it is not enough to only state that the general behavior of the national foreign policy is defined by a set of behaviors of the elements that are part of it, which actions are led by limited and individual organizational interests.

The assumptions of rationality displayed by the role players, who make decisions within the foreign policy agenda, may be limited by the following circumstances: the restrictions imposed by the inability to manage and assess every piece of information that requires a decision aligned with the rational model; as well as the mistakes made by individuals with different expertise and background, which causes important different perspectives and assessments of the environment. In regards to the content of Venezuela's foreign policy as public policy, we agree with Eva Josko de Gueron's statement:

> «...In both traditional and contemporary attempts to classify the State policies, foreign policy seems to be a specific type of public policy. It aims to make a national system fit into a transnational one and it ultimately involves security and survival of the State. As such, it has traditionally been considered as the first and most important policy in every State» (1975: 230)».

Foreign policy should be seen as stated by Josko de Gueron: a public policy subsystem that entails public and private factors as well as processes related to Venezuela's international relations (Ibid). Hence, the national interest in itself breaks down the differences between Venezuela's domestic and foreign policy.

The contemporary concepts about foreign policy produced by Venezuelan authors undoubtedly take the elements we have described into consideration. As per the social factor, Elsa Cardozo incorporates an innovative concept of foreign policy by describing it as «a policy that should be formulated and developed by the government and links us to the world, to other societies, in order to understand the interests and needs of the people, of the national society within a world in which it is convenient to work for the consolidation of a cosmopolitan community» (2001: 9). On the other hand, as per the bureaucratic aspect, Alfredo Toro Hardy (1993) understands it as the external expression of the Venezuelan national project.

Toro Hardy developed a model that was founded on the paradigm of political realism, which systematizes the elements that enable the methodological analysis of foreign policy. The significant contribution this model involves is the actual possibility of articulating the needs with the desires of a State, as long as it is based on a three-premise foundation, which is defined by the author as follows:

> «It is composed by the achievement of purpose, credibility and efficiency: a purpose to define a path; international credibility to both endorse and minimize the issues in the path, and efficiency to provide the skills to attain the previous two. These three elements are the cornerstone of every foreign policy (1993: 73, 115)»

The States will be subject to a series of conditioning factors while trying to achieve these elements. However, there are three which are crucial: The political system, the hierarchy of the State and the bureaucratic regime. Every State that desires to plan its foreign affairs in an objective and feasible manner should take these elements into consideration because they lead the development of the conditioning factors and their consequences.

Toro Hardy (1993) uses the classification suggested by Merle, who theorizes about the hierarchic level of the States depending on the geographic sphere of their intervention and the stages involved. The typological definitions of these States are as follows:

- States with a global sphere of intervention and it may intervene in different aspects simultaneously: military, political, economic, ideological and cultural.
- States the desire to achieve the status of world power but lack the skills to achieve it because of two main reasons: the first one is strictly geographical; the second one is the State's inability to intervene in different aspects at the same time, which restrains them from showing coercive power as to portray a strongly hierarchic position.
- States that have no ambition or possibilities of playing the role of world leaders; but yet have the skills required to be regional leaders.
- States that have to defend their sovereignty from a series of threats. These countries may not desire to achieve a leading status because of their weakness, but they may play an influencing role at a local level and align with a State with a higher hierarchy that can protect them from any risks to their integrity.

Toro Hardy (1993) says this classification is meritorious and relevant because it allows to prioritize the levels of influence the States have according to their degrees of power and their area of influence: technical, financial, cultural, ideological, defense, etc.

The political system «embodies a specific social power that has attained the State power» (Ibid). When the social power has achieved a complete control over its own local context, it may define its attitude for other factual powers. Factual powers are sectors that compose a social group. The attitude may be tolerance, dialogue or rejection. The social power will then have an influence on the foreign policy as the main influencer of the State organizations. It may be said that the political system may be open or closed: it is open as long as the sector that controls the State allows the factual groups to interact and talk; it is closed when the power does not accept any interference or relations other than its own conceptual line, and it only sticks to the principles and actions the group of power has previously decided to do. The only possible manifestation in it is authoritarian.

As per the bureaucratic regime, it can be considered the platform for the expression, organization and operations of different State administrations. The bureaucracy is objectively composed by all the organs of a State. They are held accountable for the execution of the public activity and more specifically the administrative activity with trained and qualified staff. Subjectively, they're public officers. Their origin is traced back to the birth of the centralized modern State but it gains full significance up to the development of the State interventionism.

According to the model suggested by Alfredo Toro Hardy (1993), the bureaucracy as a regime may manifest itself in two trends: instrumental and substantial. The instrumental bureaucracy involves a very competent bureaucrat with scientific knowledge who considers their main goal is to serve the State. In this type of bureaucracy, the public officer and the politician compose a permanent antithesis: The first one takes the role of executor as the owner of the knowledge and the second one embodies the legitimacy. In the substantive bureaucracy, the activities performed by the public officer and the politician tend to blend up to a point in which they are not easily differentiable. The bureaucrat and the politician interact through a series of channels that are not determined by rule. The bureaucrat does not keep a neutral position because their public role mostly entails obedience to the party ideology. This is why the objectives and purposes may be more easily achievable, as no conflict threatens the articulation of a given policy; the structural efficiency of the substantive bureaucracy is bigger than that of the instrumental bureaucracy.

Based on the previous statements, it is possible to say that in Venezuela, right after the implementation of the political system currently in place, bureaucracy turned substantive because there is a strong agreement on the interests of the bureaucrats who work for the State and the parties that control de power. This fusion has been changing due to the recently issued Administrative Career Law which protects the officers' stability; however, its strong influence from the president's role has caused that the jobs known as freely appointed and removable, which often refer to generally high positions in the organogram of the Ministry of Foreign Affairs, be taken by people who are extremely committed to the ideology of the party in power.

The purpose of each State is manifested through its foreign policy, in order to materialize its national project as the set of values in the life of the nation, which can either be an imposition or the result of general consensus. Besides, foreign policy is the representation of the desired country, as well as the main and formal expression of the political regime's nature.

When referring to the concept of national project, Toro Hardy says that:

> ...it is an expression of a given political regime that wishes to define its vision of a desirable social order (...) which can be formally expressed in different manners (...) it is often defined in the fundamental text or texts that provide institutional legitimacy to the political regime in power (...) it is possible it may also be expressed by government policies that involve a global design that can change the society due to its wide range of objectives (1993: 17).

The formal expression of the national project Toro Hardy (Ibid) refers to was present in general terms in the 1961 constitution. It contained the consensus between the State and the factual powers that were active back then. This was known as Pact of Punto Fijo.

The credibility is considered an underlying need in foreign policy because it will determine the capacity for response a State may expect to have in the global scenario. The credibility may also determine the possibilities of recognition, which may have an impact on how successfully a goal can be achieved. The resources used by the State to improve its credibility may be crucial to know the cost/benefit relation. This is not only implicit in every political action but also key to evaluate the results.

Real power is not the only important element in the international scenario; reputation is also relevant and also capable of influencing the acknowledgement and support or not from other States. These can also be known as the players and the «patients». The players are States with an independent capacity to intervene in the world scenario and its ability to achieve objectives. The patients are States that can only passively assimilate the players' initiatives.

Toro Hardy divides the efficiency in substantive, structural and procedural; and when applicable to foreign policy, it is understood as the «authorization or capability to achieve concrete results: The materialization of the purpose and the gain of credibility within the context of a State's international relations (1993: 137). The substantive efficiency is determined by the political orientation of the State and responds to the ideological project of the political regime. Hence the hierarchy of the State becomes a factor of efficiency or inefficiency, depending on the selection of a conflictive or consensual policy in international matters.

What seems to be logical is a nation with ethical power and regional influence such as Venezuela, finds a conflictive policy inefficient. On the other hand, structural efficiency means the capacity of the State to achieve its main purpose once sufficient credibility has been attained, so that there is coherence and balance between the bureaucratic regime and the institutional interests. Procedural efficiency refers to the rationality and coherence a State achieves to meet its targets. This should be sufficiently firm and balanced so that regardless the political regime and its hierarchy, it can still be achieved.

The study of foreign policy in Venezuela produces a result that lies in a three-premise foundation: the revision of the history and changes in the political system; analysis of how decisions were made including the personal style of whoever made such decisions (whether driven by ideological elements or simply by realistic positions); and the organizational and functional structure of the bureaucracy responsible for executing the actions. These premises will guide us to determine the importance of the topics, the orientation of each tendency and the identification of interests, which will not be elaborated on in the present piece because of its complexity and extension it would entail. It would also mislead us from our study focus on the relations with Public International Law.

Relations with Public International Law

The discussion about the role of International Law includes critics to the role it has played in the international relations. Some believe Public International Law is a set of rules created by powerful States in order to protect their own interests. A different perspective is that of those who say the rules of International Law are constantly ignored and unobserved by the nations.

Henkin (1979) says International Law is the result of the complex interaction of diverse forces in international politics, while foreign policy is nothing more but the behavior of countries in numerous relations with other countries, be them bigger or smaller. These behaviors do not only include major decisions but also minor actions such as a unilateral act or the stay of diplomatic agents in friendly foreign soil. This point, as previously discussed in chapter III, is ruled by Diplomatic Law, a branch of International Law, which shows one of the multiple links to the two disciplines.

The Law relations internationally developed between two States is determined by the rules of international matters, which are expressed in international treaties that rule the behavior of the countries. Despite the absence of a world government that can act as the head of State, there is an international society that relates the nations in the grounds of foreign policy, widely defined at the beginning of this chapter, with the purpose of keeping international order and consolidate national interests.

The notion of State contains a conceptual trichotomy: historical-political-legal. This means the construction of the State as a historical reality, which is determined by the elements of political power through rules that as well determine its inner structure of administrative action as a margin of legal international action. In foreign policy, the international agreement is perhaps the most important legal mechanism in compliance with the responsibility of complying with what has been agreed. *Pacta sunt servanda*: international legal principle that enables the international relations amongst States, seeing the relations of a nation include a series of international agreements, such as multilateral agreements on cooperation amongst the States that have added new dimensions to foreign policy and have a predominant position in international relations.

POLITICAL SYSTEMS AND PUBLIC INTERNATIONAL LAW

The study of political systems makes it necessary to at least revise how the social system from which the later political system structure was derived was initially created. Anthropological studies suggest that human societies mainly considered simpler were groups of hunters-collectors such as the Inuit, San, Pygmies and Australian aborigines. These peoples group a small number of families to create bands or nomad groups of 30 to 100 individuals which are related to each other and linked to a specific territory.

The survival groups of hunters-collectors - in areas of Africa, India and Philippines - enable to recognize the status of the social-political organization of the entire humanity. Their existing family relations do not only illustrate the social roots of our modern society but also show us the structure at a reduced scale, what makes it easier to analyze their process of political evolution.

The complex political-economic-social systems did not develop until after we had the favorable conditions for the settlement of permanent and stable communities throughout the year. Then, progress was seen in key economic activities such as the agriculture and others involving the use of land and animals. That is how the foundation for the development of relations amongst the humans up until the birth of the Nation-states was settled, topic we have referred to in prior chapters of this book. What follows is an approach to the definition of political system and its relation with Public International Law.

Political System

A vast bibliography refers to the definition of political system, which is why we have decided to contribute with ours without disregarding the variables that produce it. We believe a political system is created by the interaction amongst social, political, economic and cultural factors in a Nation-State to lead the political program and the national project, in regards to the structure they have chosen. The term is currently used to talk about the different types of political regimes that were born in the Middle age's Greek philosophy.

Based on a comparative study amongst different Greek cities, Aristotle[30] identified three fair forms of government (monarchy, aristocracy and polyarchy - a minor version of democracy) in his treatises *Nicomachean Ethics* (1985) and *The Politics* (1986), as well as his corresponding corrupt forms (tyranny, oligarchy and demagogy). Similar to what was written by Aristotle we can find the political assumptions by Jean-Jacques Rousseau[31], amongst we'd like to refer to *The Social Contract* (1997), a piece in which he identifies three forms of government depending on the number of governors: democracy, in which «the people or most of the people» exercises their sovereignty; aristocracy, in which «it is defined by a minority»; and monarchy, in which the government is centered in the hands of only one ruler whose power everyone else is subdue to». Rousseau says that «each form of government is the best in some cases and the worst in others» (1997: 35).

Contemporary political science identifies three types of political organization: pluralist democracies, authoritarian regimes and totalitarian systems. The first one legitimizes the disagreements, the second one prohibits their public expressions and the third one attempts to exterminate them by remodeling the mental structure.

Relations with Public International Law

All political systems may be related to Public International Law depending on the relations between their domestic laws and International Law. As previously studied when we approached the dualist and monist theories, political systems legitimize International Law in their domestic system and at the same time contribute with the construction of the Domestic Law that will be used in their international environment. For example, an approbatory law for an international treaty is brought up to the legislative body as a result of the political exercise within the internal system. Legislators are the people's representatives, but they also are a political piece representing a party or a project that can only work in democratic or alternative regimes. This relation is determined by two variables: the consistency of the structure of a nation's internal power and the international impact of the conventional norm that is to be implemented.

---

30 Greek philosopher (384 - 322 B.C.).

31 Illustrated French philosopher (Geneva, 6/28/1712; Ermenonville 2/7/1778).

Conclusion

The comprehension process of any science requires the previous review of concepts and principles which produce bodies of knowledge. Public International Law is immersed in this reality. The analysis we have done links the legal, social and political concepts on a historic base that grants it specificity. By reviewing the concept of Public International Law, we were able to identify certain elements that have changed due to the exposing factors and the weakness shown in the latest would events. The definition of Public International Law as an imperfect international juridical system, with a conventional character, is originated by understanding, analyzing and interpreting the concepts we have revised trough an undeniable reality. The use of force over the juridical provisions, international treaties and agreements shows the need to amend certain international procedures as they do not adjust themselves to the turbulent times we are facing. The existence of new political phenomena constituted of sources of International Law, since subjects were given obligations and duties, are full expression of the changes dynamic and the necessity for renovation.

Diplomacy is an instrument applicable to Public International Law, which is a reason why it is necessary to invoke the principle of sovereign equality in order to make the weak nations voices taken into consideration through their Heads of states. If not achieved, it cannot be talk about international justice as a maximum desire of societies ruled by the supremacy of law.

FUNDAMENTALS OF PUBLIC INTERNATIONAL LAW. INTRODUCTION TO THE STUDY OF PUBLIC INTERNATIONAL LAW INSTITUTIONS' HISTORY AND ITS IMPACT ON INTERNATIONAL RELATIONS of LUIS MANUEL MARCANO SALAZAR
was printed in the Republic of Argentina in January 2020.

www.ingramcontent.com/pod-product-compliance
Lightning Source LLC
Chambersburg PA
CBHW022105240926
51848CB00008B/147
* 9 7 8 9 5 6 3 9 2 7 7 5 7 *